In the Name of Allah,
The Merciful, The Most Beneficent

The Divine
Nature

Yassin Roushdy

ISBN : 1 87 0582 31 4

Edited by Abdalhaqq Bewley and Muhammad Isa Waley

Production: Bookwork, Norwich

Published by:
    Dar Al Taqwa Ltd.
    7A Melcombe Street
    Baker Street
    London NW1 6AE
    email : dar.altaqwa2btinternet.com

Printed and bound by :
    De-Luxe Printers
    245a, Acton Lane
    London NW10 7NR
    website : http://www.de-luxe.com
    email : printers@de-luxe.com

Table of Contents

i

iii

Preface

The greatest knowledge one can have is knowledge of Allah. That is why I present to you this humble attempt to convey something of this knowledge.

The topic of this book is an interesting yet intricate one – discussing it is complex and not easy. In doing so I can only ask Allah for His aid and beg His forgiveness for any faults or mistakes I may make. Only Allah – glory be to Him – is able to describe the true Essence of His Exalted Self.

I was also keen to present a thorough summary of all the viewpoints of our forebears, the early believers, concerning this subject, which is the Oneness, Attributes and Actions of Allah, so that in expressing my own opinion and quoting the most acceptable viewpoints from the past it might be possible to uncover to the greatest possible extent the lights of this knowledge, though these lights will increase day by day, generation after generation, through the efforts of the scholars of the Muslim nation until Allah – praise and glory be to Him – inherits the earth and everyone on it.

All that the early believers said, and also what present and future believers may say, can never be more than a feeble attempt in the face of the vastness of this matter. May Allah Almighty accept and reward these efforts and pardon any errors. We can only acknowledge our inability and lack of knowledge. No one save Allah has true knowledge of Allah.

The studies that have been made concerning this topic started among the wives of the Prophet, may Allah bless him and grant him peace, such as Umm Salama, and his Companions, may Allah be pleased with them all, who were the ones closest to the Prophet. Among those who studied this subject are also the four famous Imams and Nu'aym ibn Hammad who was the teacher of al-

1

Bukhari who is the most acknowledged collector of the *Hadith*, Sufyan ath-Thawri, Ibn al-Mubarak, Ibn 'Uyayna, Waki', who was the teacher of Imam Malik, Muhammad ibn al-Hasan, al-Bukhari, Ibn Taymiyya, Ibn al-Qayyim, al-Baghawi, ar-Razi, al-Jalalayn, al-Alusi, and many other scholars who studied the *Hadith* and the interpretation of the Qur'an.

May Allah forgive all our sins and accept our efforts and reward us with the best of rewards. He is the One who hears all things and responds to those who supplicate Him.

Yassin Roushdy

The Logical Proof
of the Existence of Allah

Existence

Things may exist at three levels. If they are visible they have original true existence; if they are grasped by our minds they have formative, acknowledged existence; and if they are expressed in words they have verbal, referential existence. Verbal referential existence expresses the formative acknowledged existence that embodies the original true existence.

If things were not perceptible they could not have been conceivable as images by our minds; if they had not been grasped by our minds human beings could not have been aware of their existence; and hence they could not have been expressed in words.

The word, knowledge and the known

These three things, though ostensibly different, are in reality identical and parallel although each one has its specific characteristics, just as in the case of the name, the named, and the naming.

God's Name is Allah; the Named – glory be to Him – is the Divine Unity; and as for the naming, it has been done either by the people or by Himself but in either case the Name has been known and acknowledged since eternity. When Allah inspired mankind to utter His Name, His verbal existence was thus established. His Name is eternal so far as formative, acknowledged existence is concerned because it has been known to Him since eternity, but so

3

far as His verbal existence is concerned it is dependent on His Name being enunciated by people.

Divisions of the Known

Verbal referential existence leads necessarily to formative acknowledged existence. The word 'Allah' connotes Allah's existence in our minds. Any word denotes a known thing that falls into one of the following three categories.

- **The Impossible in Itself:** This is that whose non-existence depends upon no cause other than its own impossibility, such as the impossibility of the existence of two contradictory elements at the same time. We cannot posit the existence and the non-existence of one thing at the same time, for this is unacceptable to the intellect. The Impossible cannot exist in minds nor in reality.

- **The Possible in Itself:** This is that whose existence and non-existence are due to specific causes. All existing things perceptible by our senses are examples of the possible in itself: they need a cause to exist and another to cease to exist. The existence of the cause must precede that of the possible. Anything that is preceded by non-existence can only be contingent; hence the possible is contingent because it is preceded by non-existence.

  Possible things not only need a cause to exist: they also need a cause to continue to exist. That cause is the Originator, the Donor of existence, and the true Doer, which bestows existence upon those possible things.

  Since the Possible needs a cause to exist it must have an original Source. That Source cannot be an impossible; nor can it be another possible, since that would itself need an original Source. Hence it can only be that Necessary Existent Whose Existence is the true cause of all existence.

4

- **The Necessary Existent:** this is that which is self-existent and whose existence is not due to any other cause but its own presence and attributes.

The essential Attributes of the Necessary Existent

- It must be eternal. If we posited otherwise, it would mean that It would have a period of non-existence; but anything whose existence is preceded by a period of non-existence is contingent and therefore needs a cause to endow it with existence. If the Necessary Existent were not eternal it would need an originator; but this is impossible because the Necessary Existent is that which is self-existent and so by definition needs no cause to endow it with existence, being itself the originator of all existing things.

- Non-existence cannot be predicated for it because in that case it would be deprived of itself and this is impossible.

- It cannot be composed of parts, because if that were so it would require the prior presence of those parts, which would therefore need independent existence. Hence it would need the existence of something else – whereas the existence of the Necessary Existent is not due to any cause save itself.

- It cannot be divisible, for if it were divisible the result would be a number of separate parts and that is impossible, as has been shown above.

- It must be omniscient. Its all-inclusive knowledge must precede every acknowledged thing since otherwise the acknowledged entity would exist independently of the knowledge of the Necessary Existent, which is impossible.

- It must have absolute power in order to be able to originate and create all possible and potential things and the means of their existence and survival as well as the causes of their annihilation.

- It must have an irresistable will and absolute freedom of choice, because all the possible entities exist at a specific time and with certain specific characteristics and could have been otherwise. Therefore they exist according to the eternal will of their Originator and Creator.

- It must be ever-living in order to be able to bestow the gift upon life to all living things. Its life must be eternal and continuous or else its knowledge, ability and will would have been impaired; but that is impossible because all possible beings are in constant need of the absolute existence and presence of the Necessary Existent.

- It must be unique in absolute existence, with no other Necessary Existent or giver of existence. If there had been any other Necessary Existent it would be either a helper or a rival. The existence of a helper would mean that the Necessary Existent did not have absolute power, while the existence of a rival would have destroyed the order of all possible things because of the divergences in will and choice.

- Its existence cannot be limited in any way because every other existent thing is restricted to a limited space in which it must either be still or moving. Both stillness and motion are accidental and anything qualified by an accident is accidental.

- It can have no body. Since it has no limited existence it can have no body as every body must have spatial limits and must be made of a number of constituents; but all these qualities apply only to contingent things.

- It cannot be restricted in terms of dimension. All dimensions are accidental and are described in relation to the human body: above, below, in front, behind, to the left or to the right. How could any direction be attributed to the Necessary Being, if all dimensions are accidents?

- All the attributes of perfection attributable to created beings must be attributed to the Necessary Being in the most perfect manner, since it is would be totally illogical to suppose that any created being could be more perfect than its Creator.

Therefore, the Necessary Existent must necessarily be one with no partner, unique with no equal, self-existent with no rival. It must be the first with no beginning, subsisting without cessation, eternal and everlasting with no end. It cannot be a body and cannot resemble any body in either form or nature. It is ever-living, and can never be overtaken by slumber or sleep. It can never be subject to death, non-existence or annihilation. It has absolute power, having the ability to create and originate. It is omniscient, Its all-inclusive knowledge encompassing every single thing. This perfect knowledge is eternal and is not altered or corrected by events. Anything that occurs can only be what the Necessary Existent wills, and what It does not will can never happen because Its will encompasses all creatures. It accomplishes everything It wills, and nothing can escape Its all-inclusive knowledge, and nothing is beyond Its power.

This being so, the mind must perceive the essential inter-relationship between the Creator of existence and every existing created being. Knowing this relationship, it is the duty of every human being to know their Creator, their duties, and the wisdom behind their existence. The nature of this relationship can only be conveyed by an appointed mediator, because it is impossible for the ephemeral to unilaterally perceive or communicate with the Eternal. So the mediator must be selected and qualified by the Necessary Existent and must be of the same genus as the people whom he is sent to instruct. This proves the necessity of sending Messengers to reveal the existence of the Necessary Existent to human beings through legislation and conveyance after His presence has been perceived by logic and intellect.

Once the truthfulness of the Messenger has been accepted by the intellect through evidence, signs and miracles, it follows that he should be believed and listened to so that what he has to convey is properly understood. At this point the intellect's role comes to an end and the believer must totally entrust his soul to Allah and submit to His Guidance. The Prophet Muhammad, may Allah bless him and grant him peace, has informed us of other Attributes of Allah in which we must believe, such as His Hearing, Sight and Speech, and His Establishment on the Throne, which were revealed to him by Allah. *"...Nothing is like Him, and He is the All-Hearing, the All-Seeing"* (42:11); *"And Allah spoke directly to Musa"* (4:164); *"...He settled Himself firmly on the Throne."* (7:54)

The first verse affirms the attributes of Sight and Hearing and ascribes them to Allah while at the same time making it clear that these two Divine attributes do not resemble those of other creatures, being attributes of Divine Perfection. This is proved in the Qur'an by the story of Ibrahim: *"...Why do you worship what can neither hear nor see and is of no use to you at all?"* (19:42) Nothing can ever escape His Sight and Hearing. The same applies to Allah's speech – praise and glory be to Him! He is still speaking His Divine Word through His Divine Will and Power. What is said by Allah is self-existent and cannot be separated from His Exalted Self. Allah's Word follows His Will. It does not resemble His creatures' words in any way.

Allah is firmly established on the Throne, in a manner far beyond being limited by location or movement. The Throne does not bear Him, but this Throne along with the angels that bear it are subject to His Omnipotent Power. To quote Imam Malik's famous dictum: the "establishing" is well known to us; the modality of it is beyond our comprehension; faith in it is obligatory.

The Prophet Muhammad, may Allah bless him and grant him peace, also drew our attention to other Divine Attributes which are mentioned in the Qur'an: *"Say: He is Allah, Absolute Oneness, Allah the Everlasting Sustainer of all. He has not given birth and was not born. And no one is comparable to Him."* (112:1-4)

- Absolute Oneness is the attribute of Him Who is too exalted to be compound, multiple, or subject to anything which these two attributes may require, such as being corporeal or space-limited, or having a partner. The word *al-Ahad* (Absolute Oneness) repudiates the notion that anyone or anything could resemble Allah in His Essence, Attributes, or Actions. It also means that attributes of perfection can be attributed to Him alone.

- The Everlasting Sustainer: the One upon Whom all else in existence is entirely and continually dependent for everything it needs; the One, praise and glory be to Him, Who is Self-Existent and besought of all. He depends on no one, but all beings and all things depend on Him.

- He has not given birth: Allah does not need anyone to succeed Him and there is nothing that has existence independent of him.

- He was not born: He needs nothing, was not preceded by non-existence, and was not derived from anything else.

- And no one is comparable to Him: all attributes of supremacy, perfection and might belong to Him and to nothing else.

Moreover, Allah describes Himself as the Ever-Living and the Self-Existent. The word "Ever-Living" includes all the attributes of perfection of the Supreme Being; the word, "Self-Existent" includes all the attributes of perfection of His Divine Acts.

The Most Beautiful Names of Allah

Allah

The origin of the word Allah is *ilah*, which is a noun applied to anything which is worshipped. But only the truly worshipped Divine Unity is named Allah, and there are three theories about the derivation of the word Allah.

* The word Allah is a non-declinable noun because it has no dual or plural form.

* The word Allah is a proper noun designating the Divine Unity, which alone can be described by all the Divine Attributes. This all-inclusive Name comprises all the attributes of the Divine Unity. Since the Divine Unity must have a name that comprises all the Divine Attributes and since that name cannot designate anyone save the Divine Unity, it must be exclusive to the Divine Unity. It cannot itself be an attribute because if it were, the profession of faith – "there is no god but Allah" – would not be a complete profession of unitary faith.

* The most acceptable viewpoint is that the word Allah is a derivative noun. It originally denoted an attribute of divinity but became the proper noun which designated the Divine Unity alone. Now any other name must be subservient to the name Allah, so we can say that the Patient, the Omniscient, and the Subduer are some of the Names of Allah, but we cannot say that Allah is one of the Names of the Most Merciful or of the Omniscient.

Given that the name Allah is a derivative noun, it must be derived from one of the following Arabic verbs:

- *Aliha*: to worship.

- *Aliha*: to have faith in and be calm in the presence of someone: because hearts find satisfaction in the remembrance of Allah and souls find peace in knowing Him.

- *Alaha*: to become confused and baffled, as minds are bewildered when they seek to know and comprehend Allah's Attributes.

- *Aliha*: to take refuge in, as the afflicted resort to Allah and He protects them.

- *Aliha*: to be emotionally attached to the mother at the time of weaning, as worshippers are attached to Allah and supplicate to Him in times of affliction.

- *Laha:* to be veiled and high in rank, as Allah is veiled from perception and vision and is exalted above everything else.

The name Allah is the greatest of the names of the Divine Unity and the most comprehensive. Furthermore, it is said that it is the greatest name by virtue of which if the human being calls upon it, their call is answered. That is why no one else has been called by that name and this is confirmed in the Qur'anic verse: *"Do you know of any other with His Name?"* (19:65)

One of the interpretations of this verse states: Is there anyone who bears a name resembling His Name? Allah is the Name of the Only Truth, Whose existence is the only true existence; that One who combines all Divine Attributes. Only to Allah can real existence be attributed, since every existing being is not self-existent but acquires its existence only from the Existence of Allah, praise and glory be to Him.

The All-Merciful (*ar-Rahman*), the Most Merciful (*ar-Rahim*)

The All-Merciful and the Most Merciful are two bountiful names of Allah, indicating that all grace and mercy come from Him. "The All-Merciful" designates Him Whose mercy prevails over everything in this world, and "the Most Merciful" designates Him Who singles out the believers for His mercy in the Hereafter.

The name All-Merciful signifies an attribute related to the Divine Unity, whereas the name Most Merciful signifies that attribute's relationship with those on whom Allah has mercy. That is why the name "the All-Merciful" is never mentioned adjectivally in the Qur'anic verses. Allah, all praise and glory be to Him, says: *"He is Most Merciful (Rahim) to the believers"* (33:43), but He does not say "All-Merciful" *(Rahman)* in this context.

Ar-Rahman (the All-Merciful) in Arabic is a noun and an attribute. As an attribute, this name directly follows the Name of Allah in the Qur'anic formula "In *the Name of Allah, the All-Merciful, the Most Merciful,"* and it is mentioned in the Qur'an as a name in many places, among them: *"the All-Merciful, established firmly on the Throne"* (20:5); *"The All-Merciful taught the Qur'an"* (55:1-2); and *"Say: 'Call on Allah or call on the All-Merciful.'"* (17:110)

The two names *ar-Rahman* and *ar-Rahim* are derived from the word *rahma,* which means mercy. Perfect mercy is to grant favour to anything which merits it; superabundant mercy is to grant favour regardless of whether it is deserved. Allah's grace and mercy are perfect and superabundant. They are perfect because He bestows His gifts on all who deserve them, and superabundant because Allah's mercy and grace overflow upon the deserving and undeserving, the worthy and the unworthy, with needs, essentials and luxuries, both in this world and in the Hereafter.

In human terms mercy often involves a heart-rending, painful tenderness that overwhelms the merciful person, as if by doing a merciful deed he is trying to overcome his own feelings of painful sympathy. Furthermore merciful people frequently cannot provide the help they want to give. Perfection lies in complete ability to convey and fulfil the needs of the needy. The word *ar-Rahman*, the All-Merciful, signifies a quality of mercy far beyond mankind's power. Allah is the All-Merciful, Most Merciful to people: He endows them with a myriad of favours. He creates them, then guides them to faith and to every means of happiness. Then He grants to those who merit it bliss in the Hereafter. The most perfect bliss is offered to them when they beam in brightness and beauty looking towards their Lord's Countenance.

That is why *ar-Rahman* is more comprehensive than *ar-Rahim*. Allah – praise and glory be to Him – says: *"The All-Merciful taught the Qur'an. He created man and taught him clear expression."* (55:1-4) It is said that Allah is the All-Merciful in this world and the Hereafter but is the Most Merciful in the Hereafter alone.

The name *ar-Rahman*, All-Merciful, can never be attributed to anyone except Allah, but the name *Rahim,* Most Merciful, can be attributed to human beings. The Prophet Muhammad, may Allah bless him and grant him peace, said, "When Allah created this world, He wrote above His Throne 'My Mercy precedes My Wrath.'"

Even the disasters, diseases and other calamities that we perceive in this world are in reality nothing but mercy although this may not be understandable to our limited comprehension. In other words, good events are clearly full of mercy whereas 'bad' events are a blessing covered with a mantle of evil. No evil that afflicts a human being is harmful in itself and this is one of the secrets of the Divine Providence that we are ordered to believe in – the good and evil of it, the sweet and bitter.

Glory be to Allah Whose Mercy and Grace encompass every single thing. Glory be to the All-Merciful, Most Merciful. He is Allah.

The King (*al-Malik*)

The King is He Who has absolute control through His Essence, His Names and His Attributes over every existing being and is equally absolutely needed by everything. Kings in this world do not even have complete control over those under their sway; indeed, they are in vital need of their subjects' support, protection from their enemies, and healing from illness. Any kingship belonging to human beings, jinn or animals is inevitably ephemeral. The king will certainly die and every kingdom will inevitably be dissolved.

Allah, however, is the absolute King. He is needed by every single one of His creatures and He controls everything. His Kingdom is everlasting and eternal. He is the Lord of Power and Authority as He is the Creator of all kingdoms. He owns and rules this world and the Hereafter. On the Day of Resurrection all claims will fall aside and Allah will call: *"To whom does sovereignty belong today?"* When no one replies, He will say: *"To Allah, the One, the Conqueror!"* (40:16) He grasps the heavens and the earth and shakes them vigorously, saying, "I am the King. Where are the kings of the earth? Where are the tyrants? Where are the haughty?" (Related by Muslim)

Praise belongs to the Lord and Possessor of Existence. Glory be to the King of all kings, the Possessor of all that owns or is owned. Praise be to the King. He is Allah.

The Most Pure (*al-Quddus*)

Al-Quddus is derived from the word *quds*, which means purity. The Most Pure is He Who is too exalted to have any needs or defects, He to Whom all perfection and sublimity belong. Allah is exalted above even any of the perfect epithets known among human beings, and it is a miscalculation to suppose that any epithets of mankind are adequate to truly describe Allah, the Most Pure.

Allah – praise and glory be to Him – is too exalted for any description perceptible by senses or imaginable by minds or conceivable by the intellect. It has been said that anything that is imaginable and perceptible by our minds is inevitably totally different from the reality of Allah. Glory be to Allah. Glory be to the Most Pure. He is Allah.

The Perfect Peace (*as-Salam*)

As-Salam is He Who is free of fault, Whose attributes are free of any imperfection, Whose Deeds are free of all evil, and Who is the source of all peace in the entire universe. Allah's Acts are free from any evil, all evil on earth having a good aspect hidden within it. Allah, the Perfect Peace, saves the believers from His Punishment and greets them in the Home that will last forever. Praise and Glory be to Him. He is the Perfect Peace. He is Allah.

The Safeguarder (*al-Mu'min*)

The Safeguarder is He to Whom all safety and security are due, without exception. Safety is best appreciated in times of fear and danger. The true Safeguarder is He Who is able to provide every means of safety and security. He prevents whomever He makes secure from being overcome by fear. All creatures are feeble and weak, subject to all sorts of perdition and loss both from within, through disease, and from without, by means of enemies and other calamities that befall them. Allah has bestowed on us all kinds of means of security and safety, such as medicines, barricades, and weapons, and has divulged to us the secrets of utilising them. Creatures which lack these things are given other means, such as wings in the case of birds and camouflage in the case of many animals and insects.

The worst fear is the fear of eternal damnation in the Hereafter, defence against which can only be obtained by declaring, "There is no god but Allah." These are the words to which Allah guided us. The Prophet, may Allah bless him and grant him peace, said: "Allah says, '"There is no god but Allah" are My words and I am Allah. Anyone who will say these words enters My fortress and will be defended against My punishment.'" (*hadith*) That is the highest manifestation of this name of Allah.

Blessed be Allah, Whose Presence is the Source of Security for all existence, the Safeguarder of all the worlds. Praise and Glory be to Him! He is Allah.

The Guardian of Existence (*al-Muhaymin*)

Al-Muhaymin is He Who has complete control of His creatures' actions, sustenance, and moment of death and all their affairs. Allah, the Guardian of Existence, is He Who controls all affairs through His All-Awareness, Preservation and Guardianship. He is the Guardian of this world and all the worlds together with everything, great and delicate, within them. He is the Guardian Who preserves and protects every single thing, protecting it against any assault that could demolish, eradicate or violate its integrity.

If you contemplate existence you will find an exact balance. It is Allah – glory be to Him – Who by His name the Guardian of Existence holds everything in place. Praise and Glory be to Him! He is Allah.

The Mighty (*al-'Aziz*)

The word *'aziz* means "possessing great power and superiority". It also means "rare and unparalleled". Other possible meanings are "unattainable", "peerless" and "sought-after". All these different meanings combine to give the full and perfect meaning of the epithet *'aziz*.

Allah is the Mighty Who is too exalted to be perceived by any physical or mental faculty. He dispenses by Himself with everything. All might, supremacy and exaltation belong to Him. Allah has no peer to equal or resemble Him. He has absolute existence and so none but He can be described as Mighty. Praise and Glory be to Him! He is Allah.

The Compeller (*al-Jabbar*)

The Compeller is He whose Will prevails in a compelling and overwhelming way over everybody and whose grip no one can escape. The Absolute Compeller is Allah. Hands are helpless except when provided with His power – glory be to Him! It has also been said that the name *al-Jabbar* is derived from the Arabic word *jabara* which means "to set something which is broken" and "to repair things". So *al-Jabbar* is He Who mends all the affairs of His creatures.

Glory be to Allah, to Whom everybody yields and submits and by Whom everything is remedied and repaired. He is the Compeller. Praise and glory be to Him! He is Allah.

The Haughty (*al-Mutakabbir*)

People who attribute greatness to themselves look upon everything else as mean and servile. Proud people consider themselves supreme and despise everybody else. True greatness can be attributed to Allah alone. The Prophet, may Allah bless him and grant him peace, said: "Allah says: 'Might is My wrapper and Supremacy is My cloak. I will punish anyone who vies with Me for them and I do not care." Glory be to the One Who truly deserves to be called the Haughty. Praise and Glory be to Him! He is Allah.

The Creator (*al-Khaliq*), the Maker (*al-Bari'*), the Giver of Form (*al-Musawwir*)

These three names together comprise the whole creative process. First come conception and planning, then bringing into being, then forming, shaping and final appearance.

These attributes clearly pertain to Divine Action and have led people to ask whether Allah can be described as the Creator before anything was created, or in other words, whether these names can truly be applied to the eternal Divine Nature. The most acceptable viewpoint is that these attributes do pertain to the eternal existence of the Divine Unity and that He deserved the names of creation even before the creation took place. He is the Creator, the Maker and the Bestower of Forms eternally and permanently.

If it be asked how He could be described as the Creator before He created the universe, we would say by way of illustration that water is thirst-quenching even if no one drinks it. It does not actually quench thirst until it is drunk but it has the ability to quench thirst when it is in a glass. In the same way a sword is sharp and cutting even when it is sheathed but its sharp and cutting quality is only proved when it is used. Similarly an acorn is from one point of view a tree since if it is planted a tree will emerge. Then the tree-like quality of the acorn is thus demonstrated. In a similar way Allah – glory be to Him – was always the Creator even before He created anything. He is the Creator after creating, and He will be forever the Creator, the Maker and the Bestower of Forms eternally and permanently. Praise and glory be to Him! He is Allah.

The Endlessly-Forgiving (*al-Ghaffar*)

The original meaning of the Arabic word *ghafara* is veiling and concealing. *Maghfira* is the veiling and forgiveness of all of our sins by Allah's favour and mercy following His great gift of repentance. By this name Allah conceals ignominious acts in this world and then overlooks them in the Hereafter.

Ghafir, *Ghafur* and *Ghaffar* are all names of Allah derived from the word *ghafara*. Allah is *al-Ghafir*, the Forgiver of sins; He is *al-Ghafur*, the Ever-Forgiving Who forgives a multiplicity of sins; He is *al-Ghaffar*, the Endlessly-Forgiving, Who forgives again and again recurring sins.

Forgiveness means the veiling of sins and this has various manifestations.

- Allah veils and conceals the internal ugliness of the human body and adorns it with a pleasing outward appearance.

- Allah veils man's ignominious ideas and thoughts, hiding them in his heart so that no one can see them.

- Allah veils a sinner's sins even though He possesses complete and absolute power to reveal the effects of those sins on the body or the face.

- Allah's veiling of sins applies also to the Day of Resurrection, when so much is to be revealed and yet He will not let anybody know them. He confronts the believer with his sins without anyone else knowing and then changes his evil deeds into righteous ones, blots the sins out of the believer's Book of Reckoning, and causes him and the angels to forget all the sins he committed.

Glory be to the Endlessly-Forgiving. Praise and glory be to Him! He is Allah.

The Conqueror (*al-Qahhar*)

The Conqueror is He Who subdues and vanquishes overwhelmingly everything and anything. Allah – glory be to Him – says: *"He is the Absolute Conqueror of His slaves."* (6:18)

The Conqueror's means of subduing and vanquishing His enemies are amazing and infinite. All existing things in the heavens and on earth are in His Power and on the Day of Resurrection the Almighty will call from above: *"To whom does sovereignty belong today? To Allah, the One, the Conqueror!"* (40:16) Praise and glory be to Him! He is Allah.

The Endlessly Giving (*al-Wahhab*)

The name *al-Wahhab* is derived from the word *hiba* which means a gift or donation made with no ulterior motive or thought of recompense. If someone gives without anticipating any recompense and without expecting any benefit, then he is called *wahib*, which means granter or giver. All gifts are in reality bestowed by Allah, Who fulfils all the needs of the needy and does so incessantly without expecting anything in return. He is the Endlessly Generous One Who says: *"If you try to number Allah's blessings, you can never count them."* (16:18) Praise and glory be to Him. He is Allah.

The Provider (*ar-Razzaq*)

Allah is the Creator of existence and all the ways of maintaining and sustaining it. He is the Creator of living beings, and of all the means of conveying livelihood to them and their enjoying it. The Great Provider endows all existing beings with all the means that can maintain their forms and shapes. He provides minds with knowledge and wisdom, hearts with insight, souls with inspiration, and bodies with sustenance such as food, water, air and clothes. Allah – praise and glory be to Him – says: *"Truly it is Allah Who is the Provider, the Possessor of Strength, the Sure."* (51:58) *"Your provision is in heaven – and what you are promised."* (51:22) *"There is no creature on the earth that is not dependent upon Allah for its provision. He knows where it lives and where it dies. They are all in a Clear Book."* (11:6) *"...We do not ask you for provision. We provide for you."* (20:132)

The Prophet Muhammad, may Allah bless him and grant him peace, said, "If someone tries to escape his subsistence, then his subsistence, like a lion, will reach and outstrip him until it enters his mouth;" and also, "If you trust in Allah and commend your souls to Him as you should, He will provide you with the means of subsistence as He endows the birds with their sustenance. They

leave early in the morning with empty stomachs and return full."
Praise and glory be to the Provider! He is Allah.

The Opener (*al-Fattah*)

Allah is the Opener Who opens what is locked by means of His power and concern. He remedies all blights through His Guidance, reveals to scientists and men of intellect the intricate secrets of existence, and grants them perception and deep knowledge. Allah opens the gates of success to His Messengers and Prophets so that they occupy heavenly dominions. He lifts the veil from the hearts of His chosen servants. In Allah's mighty Power lie the keys of the Unseen. He opens the treasuries of His Mercy and lets them flood out over His creatures. Allah Almighty says: *"Truly We have granted you a manifest victory"* (48:1), and *"Whatever mercy Allah opens up to people no one can withhold"* (35:2), and *"Our Lord, judge between us and our people with truth. You are the best of judges."* (7:89) All Glory be to the Opener! Praise and glory be to Him! He is Allah.

The All-Knowing (*al-'Alim*)

Allah is conversant with everything. He comprehends all things in His knowledge: the manifest and the hidden, the smallest and the greatest, the first and the last. He knows the minute details of everything in existence. The comprehensiveness and clarity of His all-inclusive knowledge cannot be completely estimated or comprehended by the human mind.

Allah – praise and glory be to Him – is the All-Knowing from pre-eternity. He knows everything about His Names, His Attributes and His Divine Acts since the beginning of creation and about all the living beings that have been and will be created until the Day of Resurrection. Allah's knowledge differs from the knowledge of His creatures in the following ways:

21

- Allah's knowledge is infinite and all-encompassing.

- Allah's knowledge coincides and is in perfect conformity in every respect with the true nature of existence.

- Allah's knowledge precedes the existence of every existent thing, and is not gained through the existence of things; rather all things gain their existence through His knowledge.

- Allah's knowledge is subject neither to variation nor to alteration. It is neither increased by information nor decreased by forgetfulness.

Allah is the All-Knowing who knows everything about Himself and His Attributes eternally and permanently. This Omniscient Power is one of the attributes that are ascribed to the Divine Essence, like His Will, by which Allah originates events in their appropriate time and in accordance with His eternal knowledge. Glory be to the All-Knowing. Praise and glory be to Him! He is Allah.

The Contractor (*al-Qabid*), the Expander (*al-Basit*)

Qabd in Arabic means "contracting" and also "taking". *Bast* means "expanding, giving liberally, or granting beyond measure". So Allah takes souls from the body at death and grants them existence in it during life. Charity is taken from the well-off, and provision and the means of subsistence are given to the poor. Allah sometimes contracts or expands in people's hearts feelings of hope or fear. He holds back, if He wishes, the evil of the unjust that is intended to befall the weak.

The word *qabd*, as mentioned in the Qur'an, may also denote having control over things, as in *"...Allah both restricts and expands"* (2:245), and *"The whole earth will be a mere handful for Him on the Day of Rising."* (39:67) The meaning of *bast* may also be extending or giving with liberality, as in *"...but do not*

22

*extend (*basata*) it either to its full extent"* (17:29); *"the winds which stir up clouds which He spreads about (*basata*) the sky however He wills"* (30:48); *"No! Both His hands are open wide (*basata*) and He gives however He wills"* (5:67); *"He favoured him greatly (*basata*) in knowledge and physical strength"* (2:247); and *"...He increased you greatly (*basata*) in stature."* (7:69)

The contrast between the two attributes shows that they can only co-exist as attributes of Allah, Who is the true Contractor and Expander of all things. Glory be to Him! He is Allah.

The Abaser (*al-Khafid*), the Exalter (*ar-Rafi'*)

Khafd means "causing to descend". *Raf'* means "elevation". Allah says: *"Bringing low, raising high"* (56:3), meaning that Allah exalts the believers and abases the pagans; and He says: *"Lower to them, out of mercy, the wing of humility"* (17:24), urging people to treat their parents with kindness and affection. Allah says: *"...and lower your wing to the believers"* (15:88); *"...We lifted up the Mount above their heads"* (4:154); *"And when Ibrahim raised the foundations of the House with Isma'il"* (2:127); *"We raised some of them above others in rank"* (43:32); *"by the Raised Canopy"* (52:5); and *"Allah will raise in rank those of you who believe and those who have been given knowledge."* (58:11)

From the previous verses it is clear that abasing and exalting can be used in a concrete as well as an abstract sense. In illustration of these two names of Allah it is said that Allah – praise and glory be to Him – abases the pagans by agonising them and elevates the believers by bestowing blessings on them. He exalts His friends by bringing them near and disgraces His enemies by keeping them at a distance. Allah exalts with His favours the rank of whomever it pleases Him to exalt, and lowers by His Vengeance the rank of whomever it pleases Him to lower. He abases His enemies by humiliating defeat and exalts His worshippers through victory. He elevates the truth and abases evil. The two names are epithets of His Divine Acts and are related to His Divine Will and

Power. Glory be to the Abaser and the Exalter! Praise and glory be to Him! He is Allah.

The Giver of Might (*al-Mu'izz*), the Debaser (*al-Mudhill*)

Allah gives might to anyone He pleases and takes it away from anyone He pleases. Allah says: *"You exalt whom You will and You abase whom You will."* (3:26) He honours the obedient and debases the disobedient. He is the Giver of Might. He says: *"But all might belongs to Allah and to His Messenger and the believers."* (63:8) Whoever is honoured by Allah is mighty: *"Those whom Allah humiliates will have no one to honour them."* (22:18)

The root of the word *mu'izz* is *'azza* which means "to reinforce, support, give glory." Allah says: *"...so We reinforced them with a third."* (36:14) Praiseworthy glory is that which is attributed to Allah. Vain glory is that which is full of arrogance, as mentioned in the Qur'anic verse: *"When he is told to show fear of Allah, he is seized by vainglory which drives him to wrongdoing."* (2:206) Here the glory is disgraceful and full of arrogance.

There is also praiseworthy humiliation. Allah says: *"humble with the believers, fierce with the rejectors."* (5:57) The humiliation mentioned here is void of oppression but is voluntarily undertaken since the believers are humble to Allah, praise be to Him.

The Arabic word *mudhill* also means "to make things submit or yield". Allah says: *"It is He who has made the earth submissive to you."* (67:15) In this verse, 'submissive' means that Allah has given man the necessary intelligence and has made the earth tractable to that intelligence: *"We have made them tame for them, and some they ride and some they eat"* (36:72); and *"... Its shading branches will hang down over them, its ripe fruit dangling ready to be picked."* (76:14)

As for reprehensible humiliation, it is disgraceful for it is the result of oppression. Allah relates what the rejectors will say: *"...before we were humbled and disgraced."* (20:134) *Adhalla* means "to degrade, to put someone to shame, to humiliate and demean". Allah says about the rejectors of faith: *"such people will be among the most abased."* (58:20)

Allah's two names, the Giver of Might and the Debaser, are two attributes related to Divine Actions. It is noticeable that attributes relating to Divine Acts are frequently opposites, showing that the power and might of Allah are infinite. Allah bestows life and death, inflicts harm and gives benefit, lowers and exalts, debases and honours. He contracts and expands, originates and restores. He has the power to do as He pleases.

It is irrational to suppose that Allah is obliged to do anything. Human obligations have to be discharged since otherwise harm would result sooner or later; but this is inconceivable with respect to Allah because He is the One Who assigns, orders and prohibits. All that occurs in the universe is simply His making, creating and invention. He creates mankind, their abilities, and all their movements. All actions performed by any created being are, too, Allah's creation. He says: *"Allah is the Creator of all things"* (39:62) and *"Allah created you and what you do."* (37:96)

All incidents, knowledge, existence and non-existence are His Creation, are known to Him, and happen because He wants them to happen. Nothing He does is devoid of wisdom, even if it be concealed. Praise and glory be to Him! He is the Giver of Might and the Debaser. He is Allah.

The All-Hearing (*As-Sami'*), the All-Seeing (*al-Basir*)

Two of the attributes that are related to the Divine Essence are hearing and sight. Just as Allah cannot be compared to His creatures, nor can His Attributes be likened to theirs. Some scholars say that the attribute and the described are one and the same; others maintain that the two are different. A third group contend that the attribute is not identical to the described but that at the same time they are not different. The truth is that Allah's Attributes are beyond the grasp of our limited minds. We will never understand the true essence of Allah's Attributes.

Our ancestors, may Allah be pleased with them, understood these Divine Attributes in accordance with their literal meanings. They did not delve beyond the literal meaning of these Divine Attributes and they did not wade through comparisons and definitions arising from the fact that these epithets are also attributed to created beings. As Allah cannot be compared to any other being, so neither can His Attributes. We should attribute to Him only what He has attributed to Himself, without interpretation or analogy, and acknowledge the knowledge of the true nature of His Attributes to be His alone.

We should say that Allah is All-Knowing by having knowledge, Living bt having life, All-Powerful by having overwhelming power, Willing by having volition, Speaking, All-Seeing, and All-Hearing having the means to speak, to see and to hear, without our trying to imagine how this can take place.

The All-Hearing is Allah, Whose knowledge encompasses everything. Nothing can escape His knowledge even if it is secret, hidden or faint. Nothing escapes His hearing; no call can ever occupy or hinder Him from hearing and answering another call. His hearing catches all sounds and voices. He is too Exalted for His hearing to be dependent on an organ. It is an attribute by which anything that can be heard is made known to Him.

Allah is the All-Seeing. Nothing escapes His Sight, even what is under the earth. Allah sees the secrets of thoughts. No darkness or veil can conceal anything from that Divine Vision, which like His hearing is too Exalted to be dependent on any organ. Allah's Sight is a Divine Attribute by which all that can be seen is revealed to Him. No existent being, whether it is visible or invisible to others, can escape from His sight.

Allah says to Musa: *"I will be with you, All-Hearing and All-Seeing"* (20:46); He also says, *"Allah has heard the words of the woman who disputes with you about her husband"* (58:1); *"Allah has heard the words of those who say, 'Allah is poor and we are rich'"* (3:181); *"Or do they imagine that We do not hear their secrets and their private talk? On the contrary: Our messengers are right there with them writing it down!"* (43:80) *"By no means! Go, both of you, with Our Signs. We will certainly be together with*

26

you, listening." (26:15) *"Allah is All-Hearing, All-Seeing."* (22:75)

Glory be to the All-Seeing, All-Hearing. Praise and glory be to Him! He is Allah.

The Judge (*al-Hakam*)

A judge is someone who decides between disputants, as mentioned in the Qur'an: *"...appoint an arbiter from his people and an arbiter from her people"* (4:35), *"Am I to desire anyone other than Allah as a judge?"* (6:114). A judge also rules and governs, as in *"... when you judge between people, to judge with justice."* (4:58) Allah's Will is carried out according to His Plan. He says about Himself: *"...Allah makes whatever judgements He wills"* (5:2); *"...be steadfast until Allah's judgement comes. He is the Best of Judges"* (10:109); and *"...and You are the justest of judges."* (11:45) The word *hakam* denotes the perfection of what is decided. Allah says: *"then Allah confirms His Signs."* (22:52) A judge is also someone to whom people resort for judgement: *"...still desiring to turn to a satanic source for judgement."* (4:60)

The Arabic word *hukm*, which means "judgement", is related to wisdom and judiciousness, knowledge, sovereignty, and deciding between people: *"...We gave each of them judgement and knowledge"* (21:79) and *"We were Witness to their judgement."* (21:78)

The judge whose judgement can never be overturned is Allah. He says: *"Jurisdiction over it belongs to Allah alone."* (6:57) He settles matters between His creatures, decides between the righteous and the evildoers, treating every soul justly in accordance with its deeds. Allah will never break His promise. Nothing can blemish His Divine acts. Allah judges between hearts, granting them contentment and bliss, and between souls by guiding them to obedience and to the Right Way. Glory be to the Judge. Praise and glory be to Him! He is Allah.

The Just (al-'Adl)

The Just is He Who is impartial and is above inflicting any kind of tyranny or injustice in His Divine Acts and Judgements. He gives everyone their due, puts everything in its place, and administers absolute justice. *"That man will have nothing but that for which he strives; that his striving will certainly be seen; that he will then receive repayment of the fullest kind."* (53:39-40) *"The truly good will be in perfect Bliss. The dissolute will be in a Blazing Fire."* (82:13-14)

Allah's justice cannot be properly appreciated unless you reflect deeply on His Divine Acts. Anyone who contemplates will see that every single thing is put perfectly in its place; the causes and effects are set in the most perfect and harmonious pattern. The hidden aspects of the judgements of the Just are far more numerous than the manifest ones.

Allah's creatures are held, in this world, between His Justice and His gracious favours. If a human being is afflicted with misery, this happens in accordance with Allah's justice. Allah – praise and glory be to Him – says: *"Your Lord does not wrong His slaves"* (41:46); and *"Allah does not want any injustice for His slaves."* (40:31) If any good befalls one, that is a favour from Allah; as He says: *"Any good thing that happens to you comes from Allah, and any bad thing that happens to you comes from yourself"* (4:79); *"Allah's favour is truly vast"* (2:105); *"Allah's favour to you is indeed immense."* (4:113)

It is Allah who has made the believers love the true Faith. He says: *"But Allah has given you love of faith and made it pleasing to your hearts, and has made unbelief, degeneracy and disobedience hateful to you. People such as these are rightly-guided. It is a great favour from Allah and a blessing."* (49:7-8) He – glory be to Him – conferred a great favour on the believers: *"Allah showed great kindness to the believers when He sent a Messenger to them from among themselves."* (3:164) He says of the idolaters: *"Allah did not wrong them; rather they wronged themselves."* (16:33)

Glory be to the Just! Praise and glory be to Him! He is Allah.

The All-Gentle (*al-Latif*)

The all-embracing Knowledge of Allah encompasses everything: the hidden, the invisible and the manifest. Allah is All-Aware of the core and essence of things. He is imperceptible and inaccessible to our vision. He is too exalted to be restricted to space, place or direction. No mind or idea can perceive the essence of His Exalted Self. Nevertheless, He is nearer to every being than its own self and He dispels distress and worry when people are afflicted by them. He is able to mould things in a way so subtle that they may appear counter to what is meant by them. Allah knows the most minute details of every secret and all the mysterious aspects of the Unseen. Then He conveys His mercy gently and tenderly to the deserving.

When the beneficence of the Divine Acts combines with the subtlety of omniscience, this conveys the perfect meaning of the Arabic word *lutf,* which means "gentleness". The minutiae of Allah's graciousness and beneficence to His creatures are countless: *"Allah is most gentle with His slaves"* (42:19) and *"Allah is subtle in all that He wills."* (12:100)

Consider the nourishment of the foetus in its mother's womb, and then how the new-born baby knows how to suck its mother's breast immediately after its birth. Look at how the emergence of the teeth is delayed until the baby is ready to be weaned, and how the teeth are divided into molars, incisors and canines. See how the tongue is a spoon and at the same time how it is used in articulation.

Allah is the All-Gentle Who does not impose upon us anything which exceeds our capacities even though He does grant us more than our needs. Allah – praise and glory be to Him – brings out pearls from oysters, honey from bees, silk from silkworms, and the human being from mingled sperm. Consider how Allah grants man his provision without hardship, giving him all the means to utilise its advantageous elements and to get rid of its harmful elements without any human intervention. His subtle gentleness to His creatures is beyond measure. Glory be to the All-Gentle! Praise and glory be to Him! He is Allah.

The All-Aware (*al-Khabir*)

The All-Aware is He from Whom nothing is hidden whether on earth or in heaven. The All-Aware is He Who knows every movement and the apparent and the hidden aspects of all things. When omniscience interacts with the inmost secrets of things it results in absolute awareness, which is *khibra* in Arabic. The possessor of complete awareness of every single thing is Allah. He says: *"He is the All-Wise, the All-Aware"* (6:18), *"ask anyone who is informed about Him"* (25:59), and *"...I will bring you news from it."* (27:7)

The Arabic word *khabar* means in English the announcement and information with which a speaker mentions a certain event: *"How indeed could you bear patiently something you have not encompassed in your knowledge?"* (18:68); *"Allah has already informed us about you"* (9:94); *"Does He who created not know? He is the All-Pervading, the All-Aware."* (67:14)

Allah is the All-Aware. Praise and glory be to Him! He is Allah.

The Forbearing (*al-Halim*)

The Arabic word *hilm* means "forbearance, endurance and self-control". The most forbearing is He Who does not hasten to punish. He overlooks sins, forgives sinners, and grants them a respite so that they may repent. Allah, the All-Forbearing, is not provoked by the sinner's sin nor by the tyrant's tyranny. He forgives sinners although He is perfectly able and entitled to punish them as they deserve. He witnesses the deeds of the disobedient and sees them breaking His Commands but He is not overwhelmed by wrath and is never exasperated. Allah – praise and glory be to Him – says, *"And know that Allah is All-Forgiving, All-Forbearing."* (2:235) *"If Allah were to take mankind to task for what they have earned, He would not leave a single creature crawling on the earth."* (35:45)

Praise and glory be to the Forbearing Who forbears and forgives! He is Allah.

The Magnificent (*al-'Adhim*)

The Arabic word *'adhim* is used to describe anything of great stature. If one's eyesight fails to perceive the outer limits of something it must be greater than anything which can be perceived by the eyes. Accordingly the sky is greater than the earth, and the earth is greater than a single mountain. Although the sky cannot be encompassed by the field of vision the brain can gauge its dimensions. Allah is the Supreme One Who is greater than everything, Who cannot be perceived by eyesight and Who cannot be grasped by mental faculties. He challenges and disables all our faculties in their attempt to perceive Him and surpasses the utmost attempt by our mental abilities to comprehend Him. He possesses the highest grades of Honour and Glory and is never in need of any helper to do what He wills. His Supremacy had no beginning and His glory will never come to an end. He is the Magnificent. Praise and glory be to Him! He is Allah.

The Ever-Forgiving (*al-Ghafur*)

As mentioned before, the Arabic word *ghafara*, which means "to forgive", denotes of veiling and screening. Hence to forgive a sin is to veil it and let it go unpunished. Allah says: *"The Forgiver of wrong action"* (40:3); *"He is Ever-Forgiving, Most Merciful"* (10:107), and *"Is He not indeed the Almighty, the Endlessly Forgiving?"* (39:5)

Al-Ghaffar is an intensive form that suggests repeatedly recurring forgiveness. Hence it is concerned with the number of times of forgiveness. *Al-Ghafur,* on the other hand, is a form that denotes perfection and inclusiveness of forgiveness. Hence it is concerned with the attribute of forgiveness: *"Tell My slaves that I am the Ever-Forgiving, the Most Merciful."* (15:49) Glory be to the Ever-Forgiving! He is Allah.

The Most Thankful (*ash-Shakur*)

The Most Thankful is He Who gives abundantly and lavishly, even for deeds which are minute, and rewards the simplest duties. Allah endows people with high degrees and bestows unlimited bliss for the limited deeds they perform. Allah guides people to be mindful and to be grateful to Him. In the Qur'an He praises His thankful worshippers. He says: *'What an excellent slave! He truly turned to his Lord"* (38:30); *"Ibrahim was forbearing, compassionate, penitent"* (11:75); and *"They are in truth the believers."* (8;4)

Thankfulness may be shown by praise and also by giving something as a reward. When praise is bestowed by someone noble it has greater value. The more the reward, the greater the giver. Allah – glory be to Him – rewards the human being lavishly with much greater rewards than even his best deeds could possibly merit to the extent that no one could ever imagine a more gracious reward. When He praises His worshippers' righteous deeds, He praises His own acts because a human being's deeds are His creation. Since thankfulness comprises praise and reward, the Most Thankful is Allah. Praise and glory be to Him! He is Allah.

The Most High (*al-'Ali*)

Al-'Ali is He to Whom infinite Highness is attributed. Compared to Him, everything else is mean and low. Allah is exalted above having partners or rivals. His rank is infinitely great. He is Supreme over His creatures in His Power and Might. His infinite exaltedness prevents Him being grasped or encompassed by human or indeed any created mentality.

The name *al-'Ali* is derived from the Arabic noun *'uluww*, which means "being exalted". Its direct opposite is *sufl*, which means 'being low'. Both the word and its opposite have concrete as well as abstract applications. The height in rank or intellectual ability ascribed to a particular creature can only be in comparison with something else to which it is compared, so we say that something is higher than something else either in stature or in rank.

Human beings are higher in rank than animals; the living are higher than the dead; people who are chosen by Allah are higher than ordinary people; angels are higher than human beings; and a maker is higher than what he makes. In contemplating Allah's Attributes, you will find that He is the Creator eternally and permanently with no beginning and no end. He existed when everything else was non-existent, so He is by definition the Most High. Praise and Glory be to Him! He is Allah.

The Most Great (*al-Kabir*)

Allah is the Most Great in everything, for He is Eternal and Self-Sufficient. He is known to be the Most Great through the perception of the senses and the intellect. He is the One to Whom all exaltation is to be attributed. Exaltation is denotative of the perfection of His Self, and the perfection of His Self denotes perfection of existence which has two main qualities. Firstly, Allah's existence is everlasting and eternal. All other existing things are subject to a period of non-existence which inevitably precedes or succeeds their existence and hence they are imperfect. People usually call a human being whose lifetime is long *kabir*. If a person who lives for a long but limited lifetime is called *kabir*, then He Whose existence is eternal and permanent, He Who is everlasting, must be called *al-Kabir*, that is, the Great above all. Secondly, Allah's existence is the existence from which every other existence is derived. Therefore He is the Most Great. Glory be to Him! He is Allah.

The Preserver (*al-Hafiz*)

Allah, the Preserver, is the All-Knowing Whose knowledge is unalterable and everlasting. He is All-Aware of every single thing in the heavens and on earth and He preserves their existence as well. He preserves all His created beings and their bodies, with all the contradictory and opposing elements that these bodies contain. This preservation is carried out in the following ways:

- By maintaining and upholding their existence, preserving them from dissolution and extinction. Allah preserves some created things through the span of millions of years, such as earth as heaven, as well as living beings that last for decades, such as human beings and animals.

- He preserves the existence of things from destruction by maintaining a delicate balance between their contrasting states, such as the balance between heat and cold, moisture and dryness in bodies which are composed of contrary elements whether human being, animal or plant.

Human beings, for example, must maintain a particular body temperature on pain of loss of life. They need moisture which supplies the body with needed elements such as blood. They need solids to support the body's physical structure. Allah – praise and glory be to Him – combines all these divergent elements in the human body; and if it were not for His preservation of them they would repel and cancel one another out. For instance, heat would evaporate moisture and coldness would dissipate heat. Preservation gives the conflicting elements equal resisting forces, thus producing an equilibrium through which the human being's continued existence is ensured.

Preservation is also maintained by supplying whichever necessary elements are lacking. For example, when a man feels thirsty, he knows that he is in need of liquid. When he feels cold, he warms himself. Allah created a myriad foodstuffs, victuals, beverages, medicines, and other things so that if one element overwhelms another it will be neutralised by a third in order to keep a balance between all existing things, which are in fact nothing but a combination of conflicting elements. Preservation is also achieved by teaching mankind all the means of utilising these provisions which Allah created to preserve them.

Destruction can also come to any creature through internal and external factors, such as illness and enemies. Allah – praise and glory be to Him – has also given every creature the means to protect himself from these things. Every creature is endowed with means of defence, such as armour and weapons, or means of disguise and flight. What is applicable to man and animal can also be applied to plants and inanimate things, even to atoms. All the means of preservation possessed by Allah cannot be counted save by the Preserver Who says, *"...My Lord is the Preserver of all things."* (11:57) Praise and glory be to the Preserver! He is Allah.

The Powerful Maintainer (*al-Muqit*)

The Powerful Maintainer is He Who furnishes all bodily and spiritual nourishment, such as foodstuffs and beverages, science and knowledge, through which He maintains the faculties of all living things and grants them what sustains their bodies, minds and hearts. Allah's name *al-Muqit* also denotes Him Who overwhelms everything with His Power and is responsible for all things through His comprehensive and all-inclusive knowledge. Allah says – praise and glory be to Him – *"Allah gives every thing what it deserves."* (4:85)

The name "the Powerful Maintainer", *al-Muqit*, is more general than the name "the Provider" (*Ar-Razzaq*), which refers simply to Allah's power to provide all created beings with their sustenance, and more comprehensive than His Name "the All-Powerful" because not only Allah's power but also His all-inclusive knowledge are combined in the name *al-Muqit*. To preserve means to maintain the life of the living being by preserving its faculties, and He Who does so possesses power over all things because He has complete control of their lives. The Doer of all these things is Allah, the Powerful Maintainer. Praise and glory be to Him! He is Allah.

The Reckoner (*al-Hasib*)

The Arabic verb *hasaba* means "to reckon or number". Allah – praise and glory be to Him – says, *"The sun and the moon both run with precision."* (55:6) This verse tells us that in the universe there are exact mathematical laws which bear witness to Allah's Wisdom. He also reckons what His people do in order to reward them for their good deeds: *"He shall be given an easy reckoning."* (84:8) Allah is the Reckoner, for all creatures will be called to account at the same time: *"...he will be given an easy reckoning"* (6:62) and nobody but Allah can do this.

The words *husban, yahtasib, hasb,* and *hasib* are also derived from the same verb *hasaba.* The general meaning of the word *husban* is any punishment by way of reckoning as in *"...it may well be my Lord will give me better than your garden and send down on it a fireball (by way of reckoning) from the sky* (18:40), where the implied punishment is that of a thunderbolt. *Yahtasib* means "to imagine or reckon". It sometimes also means "to expect", as in *"He may provide for him from where he does not expect."* (65:3) *Hasb* means "sufficient protector", as in: *"But if they turn away, say 'Allah is enough for me.'"* (9:129) *Hasib* means "reckoner" and "judge", as in *"Allah is sufficient as a reckoner"* (4:6), *"...Today your own self is reckoner enough against you!"* (17:14)

The Reckoner is He Who grants all His creatures everything they need, and this attribute is unimaginable in respect of anyone but Allah. Every existing being is in need of what suffices it to maintain and perfect its existence. Allah is the Sufficer for everything and it is only by His mercy that things exist, endure and are made complete. If all means are sufficient, such as mother's milk for the infant, food for the adult, air for breathing, and money for the wealthy, then one must believe that the Creator of all these means is Allah, praise and glory be to Him. It is He alone Who grants everyone and everything enough to maintain their existence, and He alone is able to reckon and requite the actions of every creature on the Day of Reckoning. Praise and glory be to the Reckoner! He is Allah.

The Majestic (*al-Jalil*)

The Majestic, *al-Jalil,* is He Who is perfect in His Attributes; the Most Great is He Who is perfect in His Self, whereas the

Supreme is the One who is perfect in Both. Allah is unparalleled. He has no partner or equal in Himself, His Attributes, or His Actions. He is the Exalted One. All beauty, perfection, sublimity, and splendour are but glimpses of His Light and traces of His Sublime Attributes. Therefore, to look at His Sublime Countenance on the Day of Resurrection is something far greater than all the bliss of Paradise. *"Blessed be the Name of your Lord, Master of Majesty and Generosity."* (55:78) Glory be to Allah, the Lord of Majesty and absolute greatness! He is Allah.

The Generous (*al-Karim*)

The Generous, *al-Karim*, is He Who forgives sinners, even though He is capable of punishing them, and Who never breaks His Promise when He promises. He listens and responds to the call of the suppliant when he calls on Him. Allah never fails anyone who resorts to Him and no hope can ever exceed His Power. He frequently gives without being asked. He does not care how lavishly He gives nor to whom He grants. He forbids that anyone be called on but He.

Al-Akram, which means "the Most Generous", is the elative adjective of *al-Karim*, which means "the Generous". Allah – praise and glory be to Him – says: *"Recite: And your Lord is the Most Generous."* (96:3) He is the Lord of giving and generosity. He honours His created beings with His abundant favour and grants His abundant blessings to whomever He chooses.

Allah Almighty mentions in the Qur'an what one believer said: *"He said, 'If only my people only knew how my Lord has forgiven me and placed me among the honoured ones!'"* (36:26-27) Anyone who is deprived of Allah's honour will never be honoured by anyone: *"Those whom Allah humiliates have no one to honour them."* (22:18)

He is, and will eternally remain, the Generous. He says: *"Everyone on the earth will pass away. But the Face of your Lord will remain, Master of Majesty and Generosity."* (55:26-27). Glory be to the Generous! He is Allah.

The Watchful (*ar-Raqib*)

Allah watches and observes all things and nothing can escape Him: *"Allah is watchful over everything."* (33:52) He does not miss a thought, and not the weight of a single atom can escape Him or His knowledge, no matter whether it be in a rock, in the heavens, or on the earth. No slumber or sleep overtakes Him. Allah's watchfulness is eternal and permanent. This can only be accomplished by the Watchful. Glory be to Him! He is Allah.

The All-Responsive (*al-Mujib*)

The All-Responsive is the One Who answers the prayer of the suppliant when he calls on Him. Allah says: *"Call on Me and I will answer you."* (40:60) He answers prayers out of His loving kindness, so that either the suppliant is granted what he wants, if it is beneficial for him, or Allah turns away from him evil equivalent to what he asked for. Allah Almighty says: *"He who responds to the oppressed when they call upon Him and removes their distress."* (27:62) He alone knows perfectly and fully the needs of the needy before they ask Him. He has known these needs since pre-eternity and so He has planned and created the means of answering our prayers before they are even uttered. He is the Bestower of Favours before souls call on Him. Praise and glory be to the All-Responsive! He is Allah.

The Vast (*al-Wasi'*)

The Vast is the One Who encompasses everything. He is the Most Generous Whose mercy embraces both believers and unbelievers. Allah is the Self-Sufficient One Whose inexhaustible treasures can never be depleted. His sovereignty is unlimited.

The word is derived from the Arabic noun *sa'a,* which means "vastness". It can be applied to space, knowledge and favours. The Vast is Allah, Whose sea of all-embracing and vast knowledge has no shore. If you contemplate the favours that Allah grants His people you will find that they have no limit. He says: *"Say: 'If all the sea were ink to write down the Words of my Lord, it would run out before the Words of my Lord ran out,' even if We brought the same amount again."* (18:109) *"If all the trees on earth were pens and all the sea, with seven more seas besides, were ink, Allah's Words still would not run dry."* (31:27)

All vastness, no matter how extensive it is, must have a limit. Only the vastness of Allah's generosity is absolutely limitless. He says: *"Truly Your Lord is Vast in forgiveness"* (53:32), *"My mercy extends to all things"* (7:156) and *"His Footstool encompasses the heavens and the earth."* (2:255) Allah's knowledge encompasses everything, His Might overwhelms and subdues everything, and His mercy embraces everything – as do His generosity, might, strength and beneficence. Praise and glory be to the Vast! He is Allah.

The All-Wise (*al-Hakim*)

A wise person is someone who has wisdom, and wisdom is the best knowledge of the best of sciences. Wisdom also denotes good management of things, and supreme skill, and the art of putting things in the right place at the right time. Allah, the All-Wise, is the possessor of absolute wisdom and knowledge. He – praise and glory be to Him – knows the most exalted things of the holiest sciences, for He knows His Exalted Self, His Attributes and His Most Beautiful Names.

His knowledge is permanent. Nothing can ever deplete or escape His all-embracing knowledge, which is free from all doubt. As for the good management and mastery of all things, Allah Almighty says: *"He Who has created all things in the best possible way"* (32:7); *"The handiwork of Allah Who gives everything its solidity"* (27:88), *"Blessed be Allah, the Best of Creators!"* (23:14), and *"...Our Lord is He who gives each thing its created form and then guides it."* (20:50) Praise and glory be to the All-Wise! He is Allah.

The Loving (*al-Wadud*)

The word *wadud* is derived from *wadda*, which means "to love dearly". Allah says: *"As for those who believe and do right actions, the All-Merciful will bestow His love on them."* (19:96) The love mentioned in this verse is His love for them and their love for Him. He also says: *"You will not find people who believe in Allah and the Last Day having love for anyone who opposes Allah and His Messenger, though they be their fathers, their sons, their brothers or their clan."* (58:22) *"He is the Ever Forgiving, the Loving."* (85:14)

The love of Allah for His creatures is immeasurable. He bestows His love on His creatures by giving them knowledge of Him. His love for sinners is clothed in forgiveness and His love for all creatures is shown by giving them their sustenance. He loves the believers who love Him and He is pleased with those who perform deeds of righteousness and so He praises them for their deeds.

The name *al-Wadud*, the Loving, is close in meaning to *ar-Rahim*, the Most Merciful, yet mercy is the bestowing of goodness and blessings to the one on whom Allah has mercy. The Divine Acts of the Most Merciful are directed and granted to the feeble and the needy. On the other hand, the Divine Acts of the Most Loving do not suggest that alone: everything that Allah bestows comes from His love. He says: *"Allah will bring forward a people whom He loves and who love Him."* (5:57)

Allah, the Loving, loves them first and then He grants them the ability to love Him. "When Allah loves one of His creatures, He summons Jibril and says, 'O Jibril, I love this person, so love him!' So Jibril loves that person. Then he says to the Exalted Assembly: 'Allah Almighty loves this person, so love that person.' So the Exalted Assembly loves him and then his love will enter the heart of everybody on earth." (Related by al-Bukhari) Allah, glory be to Him, says: *"My Lord is Most Merciful, Loving."* (11:90) Glory be to the Loving, whose gifts are lavish and vast. Praise and glory be to the Loving! He is Allah.

The All-Glorious (*al-Majid*)

Allah, *al-Majid*, is the sole possessor of perfect and complete honour and of all the immense, vast dominion of existence, eternally and permanently. He is absolutely perfect in Glory and Honour. He is Exalted in rank, His Divine Acts are full of goodness, and His giving is lavish and abundant. When honour combines with goodness in an act it is called glory. Glory is attributed to Allah from pre-eternity. He, the Most Glorious, says: *"He is Praiseworthy, All-Glorious"* (11:73) and *"the All-Glorious Lord of the Throne."* (85:15) He described His words in the Qur'an, saying: *"Qaf. By the Glorious Qur'an!"* (50:1) because the Qur'an is very useful and beneficent, and because as He described it, *"Inscribed on Honoured Pages, exalted, purified."* (80:13-14) Glory be to the All-Glorious! He is Allah.

The Resurrector (*al-Ba'ith*)

The Arabic verb *ba'atha* mean "to send". Allah Almighty says: *"Your Lord knows best how long you have been here. Send one of your number into the city with this silver you have, so he may see which food is purest and bring you some of it to eat"* (18:19); *"Then after him We sent Messengers to their people."* (10:74) He sent messengers with laws and guidance. He says: *"...Then Allah sent forth Prophets bringing good news and giving warning."* (2:213)

The word *ba'atha* also means "to awaken someone up from sleep." Allah says: *"It is He Who takes you back to Himself at night, while knowing the things you perpetrate by day, and then wakes you up again, so that a specified term may be fulfilled."* (6:60) He - glory be to Him - said about the Companions of the Cave: *"Then We woke them up again so that We might see which of the two groups would better calculate the time they had stayed there."* (18:12)

Allah Almighty resurrects the dead by bringing them out of their graves and will restore them to life again on the Day of

Judgement. He says: *"As for the dead, Allah will raise them up, then to Him they will be returned."* (6:36) *"On the Day Allah raises up all of them together they will swear to Him just as they have sworn to you and imagine they have something to stand upon."* (58:18) *"Then We brought you back to life after your death."* (2:56) We are told what the dead will say after their resurrection: *"Alas for us! Who has raised us from our resting-place?"* (36:52)

Allah, the Resurrector, will resurrect creatures on the Day of Rising and reveal what is locked up in their hearts, and He will raise up those who are in the grave. He also raises souls from the death of unbelief to the life of faith in Him. He raises all existing things from the darkness of non-existence to the light of existence.

Resurrection is regeneration after death, whereas the present life is the first creation. Allah says: *"...and to re-form you in a way you do not know. You have known the first formation. So why do you not pay heed?"* (56:61-62)

We cannot fully understand what "the Resurrector" signifies unless we know the meaning of the last creation; and that is impossible until it actually happens. Therefore no one knows the true essence of the Lord of Resurrection except Allah. Praise and glory be to Him! He is Allah.

The Witness (*ash-Shahid*)

The verb *shahida* means "to witness, to be present and notice, or to say or do something in order to give evidence." Allah says: *"Any of you who are present for the month should fast it"* (2:185) and *"A witness from her people then declared..."* (12:26) *Shahida* also means "to swear and take an oath": *"...the legal proceeding of such a one is to testify four times by Allah that he is telling the truth."* (24:6) Allah Almighty says: *"...when a witness from the Tribe of Israel testifies to its similarity and believes"* (46:10); *"...witnessing what they did to the believers"* (85:7); *"You do not engage in any matter or recite any of the Qur'an or do any action without Our witnessing you while you are engrossed in it"* (10:61); *"The witnesses will say, 'Those are the ones who lied against their*

Lord.' Yes indeed! Allah's curse is on the wrongdoers'" (11:18);
"...neither writer nor witness should be put under pressure"
(2:282); and "...so write us down among the witnesses" (3:53),
that is to say, among those who assert their belief in Allah.

Ashhada means "to make someone testify or bear witness", as
in "...and made them testify against themselves: 'Am I not your
Lord?' They said, 'We testify that indeed You are!'" (7:172); and
"Call witnesses when you trade." (2:282)

Ashhada also means to make someone present at the time of
something occurring, in order to make him notice it and testify.
Allah Almighty says: "I did not make them witnesses of the creation of the heavens and the earthm nor of their own creation"
(18:51) and "That is a Day which will be witnessed by everyone"
(11:103) on which all the creatures will be present and will witness
its horrors, and the angels will also be present. Special testimony is
borne by the angels who witness and record the believers' reward,
"...and also the recitation at dawn. The dawn recitation is indeed
witnessed." (17:78)

The word *mashhad* means the time or place at which the evidence is taken, or at which people are produced to be judged. It is
a noun of time and place. Allah says: "Woe to those who reject, for
their attendance on a terrible Day!" (19:37) *Ash-Shahid* means
the Witness Who sees, observes and witnesses every single thing.
Nothing escapes Him in His Kingdom: "Is it not enough for your
Lord that He is a witness of everything?" (41:53) Allah Almighty
decides between people in the most just way, He says: "Say,
'What thing is greatest as a witness?' Say, 'Allah: He is Witness
between me and you.'" (6:19)

Allah is the Omniscient, the All-Aware and the Witness. He is
the Omniscient because His knowledge is absolute and eternal.
Inasmuch as this supreme mastery over all things combines with
knowledge of the inmost invisible secrets, then He is the All-
Aware. When all these things intermingle with knowledge of manifest matters, then He is the Witness. Allah says – praise and glory
be to Him – "Allah is Witness of everything." (58:6) He is the
Witness of all things on the Day of Judgement. Glory be to Him!
He is Allah.

The Truth (*al-Haqq*)

Al-Haqq means "the Truth", which denotes the undoubted evidential reality. The Arabic verb *haqqa* means that something is proved or made manifest, as mentioned by Allah Almighty: *"I am duty bound to say nothing about Allah but the Truth"* (7:105) whereas *haqiq* means "true, worthy of something, or devoted to it". He says: *"The Undeniable! What is the Undeniable?"* (19:1-2); it is the sure reality or truth, the event that must inevitably come to pass, the state in which all falsehood and pretence will vanish, and the absolute truth will be laid bare.

Al-Haqq may also mean "the Qur'an, justice, truthfulness, wisdom, resurrection and the perfection of things". Allah - praise and glory be to Him, says: *"The Great Blast seized them inexorably"* (23:41); *"It is He Who created the heavens and the earth with truth"* (6:73); *"How could we not believe in Allah, since the truth has come to us?"* (5:87); *"They deny the truth each time it comes to them"* (6:5); and *"They are in truth the believers."* (8:4)

Things are distinguished by their opposites: everything that we are informed of is either exclusively false or exclusively true, or else it may be false from one viewpoint and true from another. What is absolutely false is that which is impossible because of its nature; what is absolutely true is that which cannot fail to be. Allah, praise and glory be to Him, says: *"That is because Allah is the Real and what they call on apart from Him is false."* (22:62) What is possible but does not yet exist is false from one aspect and true from another. In other words, what does not exist is false and untrue, but once it comes to exist (that is, when Allah creates it) it becomes true. Non-existence is false. What comes to exist through the power of the Creator is true and real. From this we can see that as Allah is the only One Who has true existence and exists from pre-eternity, He is the eternal Truth. He says: *"All things shall perish except His Face."* (28:88)

Glory be to Allah Who has existed since pre-eternity! He is the Truth for ever and ever. Nothing but He is worthy to exist by itself. Hence the absolute Truth is Allah because He is the only One Who exists without needing anything to make Him exist, whereas every other form of truth derives its source of reality from Him.

Speech can be described as true or false. The most truthful of all words are the words we utter on declaring our profession of faith ("There is no god but Allah"). It is the only statement that is eternally and permanently true. So we can describe things as true if they exist, enunciated on tongues, visualized in minds, or if they are sighted and seen. Yet the only One of the name Truth is He Whose existence is eternal and permanent, and knowing Him and professing belief in His Existence is the sole eternal and permanent Truth. Glory be to Him! He is Allah.

The Guardian (*al-Wakil*)

Allah – praise and glory be to Him – manages subtly all the affairs of the believers. He alone can be entrusted with everything, since He suffices His creatures for all their needs. He perfectly protects all those who commit their souls to Him and satisfies with His generous gifts everyone who dispenses with everything save Him.

A guardian can either be entrusted with some affairs – in which case he is imperfect – or he can be entrusted with all affairs. The Guardian of all affairs can only be Allah. He is the One to Whom every minute thing is committed and entrusted. He is the Disposer of all affairs.

Moreover, a guardian usually needs to be appointed in order to have authority, but the One Who deserves, by Himself, that everything and every single affair should be committed and entrusted to Him is Allah, the Guardian of all existence. All hearts are entrusted to Him. Most guardians only fulfil some of the affairs committed to them but Allah suffices all the needs of all His creatures without the slightest defect.

Allah protects His creatures, for He is the Guardian. He says: *"Those to whom people said, 'The people have gathered against you so fear them.' But that merely increased them in faith and they said, 'Allah is enough for us and the Best of guardians.' So they returned with blessings and bounty from Allah and no evil touched them. They pursued the pleasure of Allah."* (3:173-174) He disposes the affairs of those who have no guardian. He says: *"He is Responsible for everything"* (6:102); *"And why indeed should we not put our trust in Allah when He has guided us on our ways?"* (14:12); *"Then when you have reached a firm decision, put your trust in Allah. Allah loves those who put their trust in Him."* (3:159); *"Say: 'I am not here as your guardian.'"* (6:66)

The Arabic word *wakil* is derived from *wakala* which means "to entrust someone to do something", so *wakil* may also mean "the one who helps and protects." *"If these people reject it, We already entrusted it to a people who did not"* (6:89) and *"If you believe in Allah then put your trust in Him, if you are Muslims."* (10:84)

True reliance and submission entail complete dependence on whoever is entrusted to be in charge, and to be content with the consequences, no matter how undesirable. Hence He Who is truly and rightfully the Disposer of all affairs is the Guardian of all existence. Praise and glory be to Him! He is Allah.

The Strong (*al-Qawi*)

Allah is the Strong: no weakness can ever affect Him, no feebleness can ever enter His Essence, His Attributes, or His Deeds. *Qawi*, which means "strong", is indicative of absolute power and ability. When someone is capable and powerful, he is said to be strong.

Quwwa, which means "strength", can be used to denote abstract strength, like that of mind, determination and will. Allah says: *"...then after weakness He gave you strength, then after strength ordained weakness and grey hair."* (30:54) It can also denote firm will and power: *"Take hold vigorously of what We have given you."* (2:63) The angel Jibril was described by Allah in the Qur'an: *"It is truly the utterance of a noble Messenger, possessing great strength, securely placed with the Lord of the Throne."* (81:19-20)

The word *quwwa* may also have various meanings of power: *"...taught him by one immensely strong"* (53:5) – nobody knows the meaning of that power save Allah the Almighty. The daughter of Shu'ayb described Musa as being strong, as is mentioned in the Qur'an: *"...The best person to hire is someone strong and trustworthy."* (28:26) Allah – praise and glory be to Him – described Himself in the Qur'an as the Strong in the verses: *"Your Lord is the All-Strong, the Almighty"* (11:66) and *"Allah is All-Strong, Almighty"* (22:40)

If we contemplate all the forces in the universe, such as gravity, electricity, chemical reactions, nuclear energy, the power of gases, rays such as laser beams and the like, we will realise that the Creator of all these powers has a strength that we will never be able to measure. The essence of Allah's strength will never be known to any creature. Glory be to the Strong! He is Allah.

The Sure (*al-Matin*)

Al-Matin is derived from *matana* which means "being firm, unchangeable, and fixed". Allah is the One Who has perfect and invincible power. No one can frustrate His Actions or prevent His orders from being carried out. Sureness denotes extreme power: the Almighty is necessarily Omnipotent. He describes Himself in the Qur'an by saying: *"Truly it is Allah Who is the Provider, the Possessor of Strength, the Sure."* (51:58) He threatened the unbelievers by saying *"I will give them more time. My strategy is sure"* (7:183), which means that His scheme is irresistible.

The Sure is He Whose omnipotence is insurmountable and inaccessible. The Sure can only be completely known to Himself. Glory be to Him! He is Allah.

The Protector (*al-Wali*)

Allah, the Protector, loves, helps and defends His creatures who are exclusively endowed with His Grace. He says: *"Allah is the*

Protector of those who believe" (2:257); *"But Allah is the Protector of the godfearing"* (45:19); *"That is because Allah is the Protector of those who believe and because those who reject have no protector"* (47:11); and *"He is the Protector, the Praiseworthy."* (42:28)

One of the meanings of the verb *waliya* is "to protect and keep safe from harm by guarding and covering". On the Day of Judgement He is the only protection: *"In that situation the only protection is from Allah, the Real"* (18:44); *"...and the wrongdoers have no protector and no helper"* (42:8); *"...If Allah desires evil for a people, there is no averting it. They have no protector apart from Him"* (13:11); *"My Protector is Allah who sent down the Book. He takes care of the righteous"* (7:196); and *"But Allah is the Protector. He gives life to the dead. He has power over all things."* (42:9)

Glory be to the Protector! Praise and glory belong to Him. He is Allah.

The Praiseworthy (*al-Hamid*)

Allah, the Praiseworthy, is praised at all times and under all circumstances. He is the Praiseworthy since He is praised by His Exalted Self and by all His creatures eternally and constantly. To Him all perfection is ascribed.

The verb *hamida* means "to praise someone out of gratitude". Allah – praise and glory be to Him – says: *"Those who turn in repentance, those who worship, those who praise"* (9:112); He also says, *"It may well be that your Lord will raise you to a Praiseworthy Station."* (17:79) Allah, the Praiseworthy, praises Himself in the Qur'an and says, *"Praise be to Allah"* (1:2) and *"Say: 'Praise be to Allah and peace be upon those of His slaves whom He has chosen.'"* (27:59)

Allah began creation with praise: *"Praise belongs to Allah who created the heavens and the earth"* (6:1). He also ended it with praise: *"And it will be said: 'Praise be to Allah, the Lord of all the worlds'"* (39:75), which is what the believers will say when they are resurrected: *"The Day He calls you, you will respond by praising Him."* (17:52)

On perceiving the bliss of the Hereafter, the believers will say, *"Praise be to Allah Who has guided us to this! We should not have been guided, had Allah not guided us."* (7:43) These words are spoken by the believers on seeing Paradise, and on entering it, they say: *"Praise be to Allah Who has fulfilled His promise to us and made us the inheritors of this land, letting us settle in the Garden wherever we will."* (39:74) When they are saved from Hell, they say: *"Praise be to Allah Who has removed all sadness from us. Truly our Lord is Ever-Forgiving, Ever-Thankful."* (35:34)

Praise of Allah fills heaven and earth. It has been said that praise is more exalted even than the profession of faith because it encompasses faith and adds to it praise and glorification, although the truth is that no more exalted thing can be uttered than the profession of faith.

To praise is to thank someone for a favour but the praise which Allah is worthy of can only be known and perfectly estimated by Him, the Praiseworthy, who praises Himself. The Prophet Muhammad, may Allah bless him and grant him peace, said, "I cannot encompass the praise due to You in the way You have perfectly praised Yourself." (*hadith*) It was reported that when a man said, "Praise be to Allah as becomes the Glory of His Countenance and the greatness of His Throne," the angels ascended and asked Allah how they should record the man's words. Allah replied, "Write down the man's exact words until I take him back. Then he will be given a complete reward."

Glory be to Allah, the Praiseworthy as He has praised Himself since pre-eternity! He is the Praiseworthy eternally and forever. He is Allah.

The Recorder (*al-Muhsi*)

Ahsa means "to count" or "register". The root of this verb signifies counting by using pebbles, that being how the Arabs used to count. Allah - praise and glory be to Him - says: *"If you try to number Allah's blessings, you can never count them"* (14:34); *"We have enumerated everything in a clear register"* (36:12); and *"...and calculate the waiting-period carefully."* (65:1)

Ahsa may also mean "to calculate". Allah Almighty says: *"Then We woke them up again so that we might see which of the two groups would better calculate the time they had stayed there"* (18:12); *"...He encompasses what is in their hands and has counted the exact number of everything"* (72:28); and *"He has counted them and numbered them precisely."* (19:94)

Allah, the Recorder, is absolutely aware of every existing thing in perfect detail. Nothing escapes Him in heavens or on earth. He is All-Seeing of all clear and manifest things. He is All-Knowing of all hidden and invisible things. His omniscience has no limit but is beyond our perception because what He records is unlimited.

On the Day of Judgement, those who indulged in sin and crime will be surprised by what they find recorded about them. They will say: *"Alas for us! How is it that this Book does not pass over any action, small or great, without recording it?"* (18:49) Allah says about the ancient nations: *"All that they did is in the Books. Every thing, great or small, is recorded."* (54:52-53) Allah's power is unlimited. He takes account of all existing things, of the deeds of creatures, and of every single movement. He says: *"No leaf falls without His knowing it. There is no seed in the darkness of the earth, nothing moist or dry, which is not in a Clear Book."* (6:59)

Praise and glory be to Allah Who comprehends all things in His all-inclusive knowledge and records every single thing! Praise and glory be to the Recorder! He is Allah.

The Originator (*al-Mubdi'*), the Regenerator (*al-Mu'id*)

To originate is to create something which has never existed before. If something similar existed before, then this is regenerating. Allah, the Originator, brought everything from non-existence into existence. The Regenerator restores them to existence after they have perished.

50

Allah Almighty says: *"It is He Who originated creation and then regenerates it. That is extremely easy for Him"* (30:27); *"He originates and regenerates"* (85:13); *"As We originated the first creation so We will regenerate it" (21:104); "As He originated you, so you will return"* (7:29); *"Falsehood cannot originate or regenerate"* (34:49); *"...He brings creation out of nothing and then regenerates it"* (10:4); and *"...see how He brought creation out of nothing. Then later Allah will bring about the next existence."* (29:19)

The Arabic verb *bada'a* means "to create something in an unexampled and unprecedented form". Examples of origination and regeneration are countless, such as the seed and the tree, or the egg and the chicken. Glory be to the Originator and the Regenerator! He is Allah.

The Life-Giver (*al-Muhyi*), the Death-Bringer (*al-Mumit*)

Allah, the Life-giver, created life in every living being, and He, the Death-Bringer, brings death to every being that dies. Allah is the Creator of life and death. He bestows life on whom He pleases and brings death to whom He pleases. Hence life-giving and death-bringing are two Divine Acts related to Allah's Will and Power. He is the Creator of life in every living being. He raises everything to life, from non-existence to existence. Then on the Day of Judgement He resurrects them after their death.

Allah Almighty says: *"How can you reject Allah, when you were dead and then He gave you life then He will make you die and then give you life, then you will be returned to Him?"* (2:28) He gives life to the earth: *"So look at the effect of the mercy of Allah, how He brings the dead earth back to life."* (30:50) Moreover, He bestows life on hearts and souls by endowing them with the light of faith: *"Is someone who was dead and whom We brought to life, supplying him with a light by which to walk among people...?"* (6:122)

51

The Death-Bringer takes away life: *"That it is He Who brings about both death and life."* (53:44) He brings death to living beings by making them sleep and gives them life by waking them up again: *"Allah caused him to die for a hundred years, then brought him back to life."* (2:259) Allah differentiates between natural death and killing: He says *"If he were to die or be killed."* (3:144)

Moreover, we are forbidden to think of those who were slain fighting for the Cause of Allah as dead. Allah - glory be to Him - says: *"Do not suppose that those killed in the Way of Allah are dead. No indeed! They are alive and well provided for in the very presence of their Lord."* (3:169) *"Do not say about those killed in the Way of Allah that they are dead. On the contrary, they are alive but you are not aware of it."* (2:154) Anyone who kills or causes death, for instance, by hunting, slaughtering or murdering, does not in reality take life or cause death, but only inflicts damage on the body or destroys it. Allah alone is true the Death-Bringer.

Life and death are created by Allah: *"He who created death and life."* (67:2) Death precedes life as the universe was first non-existent. Allah said: *"...when you were dead and then He gave you life."* (2:28)

Life-giving and Death-bringing are possible only for Allah because life itself is a great mystery and death is a greater mystery. Forms of life in human beings, animals, plants, and all living organisms such as microbes, viruses, bacteria and minute organisms are awe-inspiring and thought-provoking. The secret of life in the human being lies in the Spirit, and the true essence of the Spirit is known only to Allah. He says: *"When I have formed him and breathed My Spirit into him"* (15:29) and *"He formed him and breathed His Spirit into him."* (32:9) *"They will ask you about the Spirit. Say: 'The Spirit is my Lord's concern. You have only been given a little knowledge.'"* (17:85)

The body's contact with the Spirit and its parting with it are two matters beyond science and human comprehension. No one can ever perfectly know the Life-Giver and the Death-Bringer save Allah, Who alone possesses these two attributes. Praise and glory be to Him! He is Allah.

The Ever-Living (*al-Hayy*)

Allah, the Ever-Living, is He for whom eternal life is reserved. His life is inaccessible to destruction, death, defects or non-existence. To the Ever-Living, absolute existence is attributed. His life had no precedent and will never be followed by non-existence.

In life, the degree of sublimity and superiority is gauged according to perception and actions. Hence the life of an animal is superior to that of a plant. The life of a human being is superior to that of an animal, as acts and perception place man in a more elevated position. The righteous believer is superior to the sinner who is superior to the pagan. Allah, the Ever-Living, calls the believer 'living' and by analogy calls the pagan 'dead'. Allah Almighty says: *"The living and dead are not the same."* (35:22)

As the ranks of life vary according to the level of perception and actions, the Ever-Living is He Who embraces all perceptible things in His awareness and to Whose sovereignty all creatures submit. Nothing can escape His knowledge. No achievement can be fulfilled save by His Will. He created perception, comprehension, hearts, judgement, discretion and assessment. He created life itself, and existence in life is derived from His Supreme Existence. Truly Allah is the Ever-Living. He – praise and glory be to Him – says: *"He is the Living. There is no god but Him. So call on Him, making the* deen *sincerely His. Praise be to Allah, the Lord of all the worlds."* (40:65) Glory be to Allah, the Ever-Living! He is Allah.

The Self-Subsisting, All-Sustaining (*al-Qayyum*)

Allah is the Self-Subsisting Whose existence is not in need of anything. He is the Self-Sufficient and All-Sustaining: everything depends on Him. It is He Who gives existence to all existing things. He can dispense with everybody and everything but no one can dispense with Him. He is too exalted to be limited to place and is far above change. What befalls created souls can never befall Him. He is Supreme in perfection and in organising His Kingdom.

This name, the Self-Subsisting, can never be attributed to anyone save Him.

Allah is the Ever-Living, the All-Sustaining. He says: *"Faces will be humbled to the Ever-Living, the All-Sustaining."* (20:111) on the Day of Judgement. *"Allah – there is no god but He, the Ever-Living, the Self-Sustaining."* (2:255) That is to say, He is the Ever-Living, the Self-Subsisting eternally and permanently.

It is said that these two names together constitute Allah's greatest Name and that if someone calls for His Help by calling upon them, Allah will help him. The Prophet Muhammad, may Allah bless him and grant him peace, said, "O Ever-Living, All-Sustaining! I am calling for Your mercy's relief!" (*hadith*)

Glory be to the Self-Subsisting, the All-Sustaining. Praise and glory be to Him! He is Allah.

The Finder (*al-Wajid*)

The Arabic verb *wajada* means "to find sufficiency in one's means, to be well off." It may also mean "to find, meet and know". The definition of the name Allah *al-Wajid*, the Finder, signifies the opposite of the one who loses. Allah ordains, finds and has everything; all things are at His beck and call. The name *al-Wajid* is not mentioned in the Qur'an, but it is agreed that it is one of His Names.

If someone lacks something he does not need then he will not be a loser; similarly, someone who has what he does not need is not self-sufficient, for self-sufficent is one who does not lack anything he needs for his existence. Allah, then, is the Self-Sufficient, for He never lacks anything He needs in His Essence, His Attributes, or His Actions. He is the Self-Sufficient Who can dispense with everything. From Him all attributes of perfection are derived and to Him all the attributes of exaltation rightly belong. He is the Finder. Praise and glory be to Him! He is Allah.

The All-Glorious (*al-Majid*)

Allah's name the All-Glorious is not mentioned in the Qur'an. The Arabic word *al-Majid* is derived from the Arabic noun *majd* which means glory: that is, the zenith of honour. When the nobility of a person combines with righteousness in actions this is called glory. Allah is the All-Glorious, Whose exalted Self is the Most Supreme. No epithet can ever be compared to Allah's eternal attributes. He is the Creator of everything and the Originator of all existing things as well as all their deeds. He accomplishes whatever He pleases and all His Divine Acts are perfect and exalted. He is the All-Glorious. Praise and glory be to Him! He is Allah.

The One (*al-Wahid*)

There are four types of oneness.

- A oneness that is delineated, can be divided, and requires a place to occupy: that is something material such as the body.

- A oneness that is delineated but cannot be divided, yet requires a locus: that is something which has essence, such as the mind or the spirit.

- A oneness that is not delineated and cannot be divided, but needs a locus: that is something which has no essence and is temporal, such as sorrow or anger.

- That absolute Oneness that is not delineated, cannot be divided, and does not require a locus: He is the One and Only, unparalleled in His Essence, His Attributes and His Divine Acts.

Allah can never be compared to anything and nothing can be compared to Him. He is absolutely One in His Divine Acts. He has no partner in any of them. He is the First and everything save Him is subject to time. He is the Everlasting and everything save Him is short-lived. He is the Last and everything save Him will end. He is the One. Allah - praise and glory be to Him - says: *"And We created all things in pairs so that perhaps you might pay heed."* (51:49) The Creator of pairs is the One and we cannot attribute to Him motion or rest, light or darkness, sitting or rising, beginning or end. He says: *"Nothing is like Him."* (42:11)

Everything other than Him has a counterpart or opposite: the sun and the moon, night and day, heaven and earth, male and female, jinn and man, good and evil, sitting and rising, sleep and wakefulness, death and life, sweet and bitter, disease and medicine, sanity and insanity, fidelity and infidelity, avarice and extravagance, length and breadth, north and south, and so on infinitely.

The only one who has no peer, no resemblance, no rival, is not composed of parts and cannot be divided is the One and Only. Praise and glory be to Him! He is Allah.

The Everlasting Sustainer of all (*as-Samad*)

Allah is the Everlasting Sustainer of all: every existing thing resorts to Him in its time of need, for His help is sought and required by all His creatures, and to His mercy they turn. He needs no sustenance but all things are sustained by Him. He is too exalted for any sort of defect. He is the Everlasting Who never perishes.

Allah is the Lord Who achieves perfection in His Kingdom, the Honourable Whose honour is supreme, the Great and Righteous Whose greatness and integrity are perfect, the Most Forbearing, the Omniscient, the All-Wise Whose knowledge and wisdom are absolute. Allah is the One Who is perfect in sovereignty and honour. He is the Everlasting. He does not have offspring and was not born. Nothing is comparable to Him. Praise and glory be to the Everlasting Sustainer! He is Allah.

The All- Powerful (*al-Qadir*), the All-Capable (*al-Muqtadir*)

The two names *al-Qadir* and *al-Muqtadir* are derived from the Arabic word *qudra,* which means ability and power. Allah – praise and glory be to Him – says: *"Say: 'He possesses the power to send you punishment from above your heads or from underneath your feet, or to confuse you in sects and make you taste one other's violence.'"* (6:65) *"It is We who determine. What an excellent Determiner!"* (77:23) *"So We seized them with the seizing of One who is Almighty, All-Powerful."* (54:42) *"...on seats of honour in the presence of an All-Powerful King."* (54:55)

Allah, the All-Powerful, possesses perfect Power. Nothing can ever incapacitate Him. He is bound by nothing. He needs no modality, mediation, tool, or specialised organ. No defect can ever befall Him and nothing can stop Him from accomplishing what He desires. He is able to create the non-existent and make the existent perish.

If Allah, the All-Powerful, wills something, it is fulfilled and done, and if He does not will something it is not done. Being the Powerful, He invents and originates every existing thing. His origination is unique, unforeseen, and independent of any aid or help.

Allah, the All-Powerful, has overwhelming power and everything is under His control. Out of His mercy and grace, He mends his creatures' lives in a way that is unparalleled. He says: *"Allah has complete power over everything."* (18:45)

Praise and glory be to the All-Powerful, the All-Capable! He is Allah.

The Advancer (*al-Muqaddim*), the Delayer (*al-Mu'akhkhir*)

The Advancer and the Delayer are two names relating to Divine Acts. Advancing and delaying are applicable to place, time, rank, and reputation. Allah, the Advancer advances some things over others in existence, and effects over causes. He advances one man ahead of another, one nation ahead of another, and centuries ahead of centuries.

Allah, the Advancer, puts forward whom He pleases in this world and in the Hereafter by endowing them with high prestige, rank, divine knowledge, obedience, piety, honour and answering his calls and prayers. He holds back those when He wills by depriving them of honour, rank, nearness to Him, love, integrity, obedience, knowledge, and guidance. Glory be to Him, the Advancer and the Delayer, Who advances and retards things and creatures according to His Wisdom! Nothing can ever happen in His Kingdom but according to His Divine Will.

Whatever is advanced is put forward in relation to something else, and whatever is delayed is held back in relation to something else. Anything that is advanced or delayed is moved forward or backwards not by its own free will or its own power but by Allah Who is the Advancer and the Delayer Who creates and chooses as He pleases. Allah – praise and glory be to Him – says, *"The choice is not theirs. Glory be to Allah! He is exalted above anything they associate with Him!"* (28:68); *"Those for whom the Best from Us was pre-ordained will be far away from it"* (21:101); *"Had We so willed We could have given guidance to everyone"* (32:13); and *"He has raised some of you above others in rank."* (6:165)

He is the Advancer and the Delayer. Praise and glory be to Him! He is Allah.

The First (*al-Awwal*), the Last (*al-Akhir*)

Allah is the First, Who preceded everything, and the Last, Who will remain after everything else has ceased to exist. He is the First without beginning and the Last without end. Allah, the First, existed alone before His creatures' existence and He is the Last Who will continue to exist and annihilate His creatures and remain for ever and ever after all else has vanished.

By describing something as "first" or "last" we mean first or last in respect to something else, and the two words are opposites. Some religious scholars have said that Allah is the First with respect to all existing things, for He has existed from pre-eternity by Himself and all things derive their existence from His Existence. He is the Last with respect to knowledge, for knowledge of Him is the utmost degree of knowledge that can be perceived by the most learned of people. Everything known to human minds is merely a step on the way to knowledge of Allah, and everything returns to Him. He is the First and the Last, for He is the Creator of the universe. To Him belongs every decision in the past and the future.

It is best to say that Allah is the First and the Last in an absolute sense. He governs all affairs from the heavens to the earth. In the end all matters will be in His Hands. No one can perfectly perceive the exact meaning and essence of the two names "the First" and "the Last" but He who is the First and the Last. Glory be to Him! He is Allah.

The Outward (*adh-Dhahir*), the Inward (*al-Batin*)

All things that exist in the heavens and on earth, organisms, and celestial bodies, bear witness to their need of an Originator Who ordains and originates His creatures and endows them with their special traits and characteristics. He, the Outward, says: *"There are certainly Signs in the earth for people with certainty; and in yourselves as well. Do you not then see?"* (51:20-21) Stars attest to His Glory every time they rise and set. All living beings attest to His Grace in providing them with their sustenance. The whole universe, with its most minute details, is but a sign and an outward manifestation of Allah's Names and Attributes.

Allah – praise and glory be to Him – is the Inward Who is veiled from the perception of sight, concealed from the perception of minds. He is the Inward Who is too subtle for the perception of senses or even imagination. He is different from all that might occur to our thought processes. He is the Outward as far as definition is concerned and He is the Inward as far as modality is concerned.

Glory be to Allah Who has veiled Himself from His creatures by His Light and is hidden from them despite His overwhelming Presence. He is the Outward, and yet nothing is more Inward than Him. Praise and glory be to Him! He is Allah.

The Governor (*al-Wali*)

Allah is the Governor who handles the affairs of His creatures and manages their concerns by regulating, organising, and commanding His Kingdom. Allah is the Lord of Power and the Master of everything. He takes care of all creatures by directing and dealing with them according to His Supreme and Exalted Will. His orders are always executed and His judgement is always fulfilled. There is no Governor but Him. The word "govern" denotes ability, management, regulation, accomplishment, and rule. All these things are entirely in the hands of Allah. He is the Governor. Glory be to Him! He is Allah.

The Most Exalted (*al-Muta'ali*)

Allah, the Most Exalted, is perfect in His exaltation and elevation. He is perfect in His dignity, superior in His Essence and Attributes and Actions. He is Exalted above any kind of defect or fault. No created mind can perceive His existence on its own.

Being exalted and high or being low applies to concrete things as well as to abstract things. Everything that is considered to be high in place is said to have spatial highness and everything that has a high rank is said to have abstract highness. With abstract things that have a degree of highness, there is a discrepancy between the cause and the effect, the doer and the thing done, the perfect and the imperfect. The cause is higher than the effect, the doer is higher than the thing done, and the perfect is higher than the imperfect. Accordingly we cannot divide existing things into

60

different grades without the presupposition that Allah – praise and glory be to Him – is in the highest grade since He is the Cause of all things, the Doer in all actions and the Absolutely Perfect with no flaw.

Living things are clearly in different ranks: inanimate and animate; plants and animals; insects, mammals and humans; humans and angels. Allah – praise and glory be to Him – is too exalted to be compared to anything else. He is the Ever-Living, the Life-Giver. He is too exalted for any kind of defect. So we must perceive the exalted highness of the Divine Unity.

Though Allah is Most Exalted His exaltation does not make Him remote from His creatures. He is Exalted, yet He is near to every existing being, nearer to them even than their own selves. His nearness does not resemble the nearness of bodies, just as His Self does not resemble the selves of His creatures. But despite His extreme nearness to His creatures, He is vastly Exalted above them by His Divine Attributes and His exaltation is not relative to anything.

Allah is the Most Exalted, the Supreme above all. He is Exalted above the partners that some ascribe to Him. He is High above all that they say, Exalted and Great beyond measure! He is the Most Exalted, the Most High, the Supreme above all. Praise and glory be to Him! He is Allah.

The All-Good (*al-Barr*)

Allah, the All-Good, endows His creatures with His lavish beneficence and does not deprive them of His beneficence when they disobey. From Him, the All-Good, all goodness, is derived. He conveys good to the needy. He says: *"He is the All-Good, the Most Merciful."* (52:28)

Allah says about people who are good to others: *"...and good to his parents – he was not insolent or disobedient"* (19:14) and *"He directed me to show goodness to my mother. He has not made me insolent or arrogant."* (19:32) Allah, the All-Good, taught us to pray and ask for His goodness. He says: *"...take us back to You* with the truly good" (3:193); He commands us to be good, saying "Help each other to goodness and fear of Allah" (5:3); and advises us by saying: "You will not attain true goodness until you give of what you love." (3:92)

He tells us what true goodness consists in: "Rather, those with true goodness are those who believe in Allah" (2:177) Allah is the All-Good. All our gifts are a favour from Him. Glory be to the All-Good. Praise and glory be to Him! He is Allah.

The Ever-Returning (at-Tawwab)

Taba means "to be sorry for wrongdoing and turn to Allah in regret, repenting, and to revert to doing good deeds". Allah says: "But if anyone repents after his wrongdoing and puts things right, Allah will turn towards him" (5:42); "Then He turned towards them" (9:118); "All who repent and act rightly are turning sincerely towards Allah." (25:71) He says about those who repent constantly and of every sin: "Allah loves those who turn back from wrongdoing and He loves those who purify themselves." (2:222)

At-Tawwab is one of the names of Allah. It means that He is the One Who accepts repentance many times. He has said – praise and glory be to Him – "And show fear of Allah. Allah is Ever-Returning, Most Merciful" (49:12); and "He is the Ever-Returning, the Most Merciful." (2:54)

Allah, the Ever-Returning, originates and facilitates all the means to repentance for people, so He warns them, grants them respite and reminds them. Then if they repent He will forgive them, and if they recommit sins He will facilitate for them all the means to repentance over and over again. If someone sins a hundred times in a day and repents sincerely every time, Allah will forgive him.

Allah – praise and glory be to Him – endows people with His Grace after they have suffered from deprivation and endows them with all sorts of good. He grants them success after defeat, relieves them when they are distressed, and forgives them. He delivers them from the humiliation of sin to the dignity of obedience and from abysmal darkness to dazzling light.

Glory be to Allah! No disobedience can ever harm Him and no obedience can ever benefit Him. He is the Provider of repentance Who guides us to it, and by means of that repentance He changes evil deeds into righteous ones. He is the Ever-Returning. Glory be to Him! He is Allah.

The Avenger (*al-Muntaqim*)

Allah, the Avenger, breaks the backs of tyrants and severely punishes those who are determined to commit sins. He avenges Himself on sinners by severely punishing them. Vengeance is the utmost degree of exemplary punishment and chastisement. Allah Almighty says: *"Allah is Almighty, Avenging"* (14:47); *"We shall avenge Ourselves on the evil-doers"* (32:22); *"Then when they had provoked Our wrath, We avenged Ourselves on them"* (43:55); and *"...if anyone does it again Allah will avenge Himself on him. Allah is Almighty, Avenging."* (5:98)

Vengeance is more severe than immediate punishment, which does not enable oppressors to indulge in disobedience or sins. Allah, the Avenger, exacts retribution after giving respite, then He tortures the culprits and severely punishes the oppressors; but this only comes about after His threatening and warning them and giving them the means to repent.

Allah avenges Himself only on high-handed tyrants. He says: *"We avenged Ourselves on those who did evil."* (30:47) Glory be to the Avenger, the Doer of all that He intends. Praise and glory be to Him! He is Allah.

The All-Pardoning (*al-'Afuww*)

'Afa means "to efface sins, to forgive, and to let a sinner go unpunished". Allah, the All-Pardoning, grants people complete

forgiveness. He says: *"Make allowances for people, command what is right."* (7:199)

In the Qur'an we are taught to pray to Allah and say: *"Pardon us; and forgive us; and have mercy on us."* (2:286) Allah Almighty orders people to forgive. He says: *"But pardon and overlook "* (2:109); *"...those who control their rage and pardon other people"* (3:134); and of Himself He says: *"Allah is All-Pardoning, Ever-Forgiving."* (22:60)

Pardoning sins is more comprehensive than simple forgiveness, for the latter denotes the veiling of sins whereas pardoning entails the complete erasing of sins along with remission. Allah says: *"It is He Who accepts repentance from His slaves and pardons evil acts."* (42:25) Moreover, "the one who repents from sins is like the one who is free from sins". *(hadith)* Praise and glory be to the All-Pardon-ing! He is Allah.

The Kindly (*ar-Ra'uf*)

Ra'afa in Arabic means "to have compassion on someone and dread that any harm should befall him". Compassion is more comprehensive than mercy. Allah's compassion is denotative of His protection of people. He removes and blots out blights with overwhelming beneficence and compassion. His compassion is prevalent. He says - glory be to Him - *"Allah is All-Compassionate, Most Merciful to mankind."* (2:143)

It is said that Imam Ahmad ibn Hanbal was informed that a man in a distant place narrated sayings of the Prophet, so he headed for that man and found him feeding a dog. When he finished, he turned to Imam Ahmad and said, "Perhaps you have become exasperated because I have been busy with the dog and have not attended to you?" The Imam replied, "Yes." Then the man said, "Abu'z-Zinad told me that he heard from al-A'raj who stated that Abu Hurayra had reported that the Prophet, may Allah bless him and grant him peace, said, 'He who disappoints anyone who resorts to him and makes him give up hope will be disappointed by Allah on the Day of Judgement and will never enter Paradise.'"

Then the man said, "Our town has few dogs, and that dog sought my help and I feared to disappoint him." Imam Ahmad said, "That saying of the Prophet is enough for me," and returned to his country.

Allah's compassion is granted to the merciful. As the Prophet Muhammad, may Allah bless him and grant him peace, said: "Allah has mercy on those who are merciful." He also said, "Have mercy on every existing being on earth and the Lord of the Heaven will have mercy on you." Praise and glory be to the All-Compassionate, the Most Merciful! He is Allah.

The Possessor of Sovereignty (*Malik al-Mulk*)

Malik in Arabic means "owner", *mulk* means "power" or "sovereignty", and the English translation of the Arabic phrase *Malik al-Mulk* is "the Possessor of Sovereignty". Allah deals with everything in His kingdom as it pleases Him. He is the Possessor of Sovereignty.

Milk, which means "possession", can be used in a literal as well as in a figurative sense. Allah Almighty says: *"They possess no power to remove any harm from you or to change anything."* (17:56) In this verse, power is alluded to in a figurative way.

Every kingdom on earth is ephemeral, no matter how long it lasts: however long sovereignty remains in someone's grasp, it will inevitably be conveyed to a successor. No matter how much one may possess, his possession is limited. Allah is the Master of the Kingdom, the Possessor of Sovereignty, the King who rules and establishes justice in His Kingdom. He possesses all things whether they are evident or hidden. Firstly He originates everything from non-existence; secondly, He preserves them; and thirdly, He manages and disposes of all His creatures' affairs.

Allah is the only King: all Supremacy belongs to Him. In His Hand lies absolute power. He commands according to His Will and decides all matters. To Him all things return and no one can gainsay His Command. He is the absolute King, the Possessor of the Kingdom, the Sovereign.

Praise and glory be to the Possessor of Sovereignty! He is Allah.

The Lord of Majesty and Honour (*Dhu'l-Jalal wa'l-Ikram*)

Allah possesses all majesty, perfection and sublimity. All majesty is attributed to Him. He is the Lord of Majesty in His Essence, His Attributes and His Names, the Master of Honour who grants His creatures honour and gifts in abundance. He says: *"If you try to number Allah's blessings, you can never count them"* (14:34); and *"We have honoured the sons of Adam."* (17:70)

Allah's Majesty is greatness, exaltation and being worthy of all attributes of praise. He is the Lord of Honour, for He has the sole right to be honoured, glorified and exalted. From Him all honour is derived and by Him alone can honour be granted. Glory be to the Lord of Majesty and Honour! He is Allah.

The Equitable (*al-Muqsit*)

Allah, *al-Muqsit*, praise and glory be to Him, is the Equitable Who is just in all His judgements. *"Say: 'My Lord has commanded justice'"* (7:29); *"...be even-handed. Allah loves those who are even-handed"* (49:9); *"Give just weight"* (55:9;) and *"Call them after their fathers. That is juster in Allah's sight."* (33:5)

Allah, the Equitable, takes revenge on the oppressive, wards off the oppression of tyrants and lets the oppressed triumph over them. He acts justly and removes every kind of inequity. One of the most significant Divine secrets is Allah's forbearance in dealing with oppressors while relieving the oppressed.

A Muslim may unconsciously act in an unjust way and may repent without finding a way to right his evil deed. On the Day of Rising he will stand beside the person to whom he was unjust in front of Allah, the Equitable, Who will satisfy the oppressed and may forgive the unjust. No one can do that except Allah, the truly Equitable.

An episode was related by 'Umar ibn al-Khattab that once the Prophet Muhammad, may Allah bless him and grant him peace, was sitting with his Companions and laughed until his front teeth were showing, so 'Umar said, "May my father and mother be your ransom, Messenger of Allah, what has made you laugh?" The Prophet replied, "Two men from my people will kneel before Allah, the Lord of Glory. The first will say, 'O my Lord! Avenge me on that man!' So Allah Almighty will say to the second man, 'Give to your brother all that you unjustly took from him!' The man will say, 'O my Lord! I have nothing left of my good deeds.' Allah Almighty will say to the first man, 'What shall you do with your brother? He has no good deeds left.' So the man will say, 'O my Lord, let him bear some of my sins and be punished for them instead of me!'"

The Prophet, may Allah bless him and grant him peace, had tears in his eyes as he said, "That will be a terrible Day when people will need someone to bear their sins." Then he said, "Then Allah Almighty will say to the oppressed, 'Lift your eyes and take a look at Paradise!' The man will say, 'O my Lord! I can see cities of silver and palaces of gold, studded with pearls. Who is the Prophet to whom all this will be granted? Who is the righteous man who will have all this? Who is the martyr who will have these things?' So Allah Almighty will say, 'All of this will be granted to the one who can pay for it.' So the oppressed will ask, 'And who can pay for it?' Allah will say, 'You can.' 'How, my Lord?' he will ask. Allah Almighty will say, 'By forgiving your brother.' The man will say, 'O my Lord! I forgive him!' Allah will say, 'Take your brother's hand and let him enter Paradise.'" Then the Prophet, may Allah bless him and grant him peace, said, "Fear Allah and promote accord between yourselves, for then Allah will make your relations on the Day of Rising whole and sound." (*hadith*)

The Prophet said, may Allah bless him and grant him peace – "Allah – praise and glory be to Him – has said: 'If you pray that someone be punished because of his injustice to you and another prays that you will be punished because of your injustice to him, if you wish, We will answer both prayers or else We will reprieve both of you until the Day of Judgement when My forbearance will overwhelm you all.'" (*hadith*) Praise and glory be to the Equitable! He is Allah.

The Gatherer (*al-Jami'*)

Jama'a in Arabic means "to collect" or "to gather together," as in *"Those to whom people said, 'The people have gathered against you so fear them.'"* (3:173) It may also mean "to make up one's mind and come to a decision". Allah says: *"They gathered all together and agreed to put him at the bottom of the well"* (12:15); and *"Say: 'If both men and jinn banded together to produce the like of this Qur'an, they could never produce anything like it, even if they backed each other up.'"* (17:88) The Gatherer is one of the Names of Allah: *"Our Lord, You are the Gatherer of mankind to a Day of which there is no doubt."* (3:9) He is the Gatherer of similar, dissimilar and contradictory things.

He also gathers dissimilar things into one thing, such as bones, flesh, blood, nerves, hair and nails in the human body. Another example is that of assembling the stem, the trunk, the leaves and the fruits in the plant.

As for contradictory things, Allah – praise and glory be to Him – brings together heat and cold, moisture and dryness in the bodies of living beings. He also combines positive and negative charges in both electricity and in magnetic forces. Even the air we breath contains oxygen and carbon dioxide.

The elaboration of the power of Allah, the Gatherer, cannot be perfectly known without knowing the details of every compound form in His Creation. Allah, the Gatherer, cannot be perfectly known save by Him. Glory be to Him. Praise and glory be to the Gatherer! He is Allah.

The Rich beyond need (*al-Ghani*)

In Arabic, *ghani* means "possessing much wealth". It also means "to dispense with people, to be independent and to be free from want".

When Allah, the Rich beyond need, suffices someone this means that Allah has enriched him so that he can do without anybody and anything: *"The only reason that they were vindictive was that Allah and His Messenger enriched them from His bounty"* (9:74); *"Did He not find you impoverished and enrich you?"* (93:8); and *"So they rejected and turned away. But Allah is completely independent of them."* (62:6) The only truly Rich One is Allah. He says: *"Your Lord is the Rich beyond need, Possessor of mercy"* (6:113); and *"O mankind! You are the poor in need of Allah, and Allah is the Rich beyond need, the Praiseworthy."* (35:15)

Allah is independent of everybody and everything. Everyone is in urgent need of Him and the grace that He bestows. It is He Who is needed by everybody and it is He Who is Rich beyond need of anything else in His Essence, His Attributes and in His Actions. He existed when nothing was with Him. Glory be to the Rich beyond need. Praise and glory be to Him! He is Allah.

The Enricher (*al-Mughni*)

Aghna means to enrich someone, fulfilling his needs so that he need not resort to anybody else. Allah is the Enricher Who enriches His creatures with all they need and gives to them lavishly. He says: *"...the giving of your Lord is not restricted."* (17:20)

A sense of self-sufficiency is one of the greatest gifts that can be bestowed upon a human being. Anyone who abstains from what is forbidden will be endowed with all the means he needs. Anyone who does without people will be enriched by Allah. Anyone who forbears will be granted forbearance, and whoever seeks the righteous way will be perfectly guided to it. Allah enriches people by

69

making them independent of everyone save Him. In reality we need no one but Allah.

Those enriched by the Enricher can never be completely self-sufficient since they inevitably need other things. They need medicines when they are ill. They need air to breathe. They need a place to live in. They need warmth and sympathy. They need a mate. Above all they need the Enricher, Who Himself needs nothing. Glory be to Allah Who enriches and suffices the human being. True is the word of Allah the Enricher when He says: *"Allah is the Rich; you are the poor."* (47:38) Praise and glory to Him! He is Allah.

The Defender (*al-Mani'*)

Allah, the Defender, fends off all causes of destruction and loss from our bodies, wealth and religion. He also deprives whomever He wills of His gifts and favours. Anything that is prevented by Him can never be brought about by someone else. Allah is the Creator of all means of defence and preservation. Allah, praise and glory be to Him, grants to everything what will benefit and preserve it against all that might spoil or damage it, and this is done in the way that becomes His Divine Will. He suffices those He pleases and deprives those He pleases by imposing trials upon them. He enriches and impoverishes, grants and deprives, blesses and distresses. He is the Granter and He is the Defender.

Poverty is sometimes more appropriate to a particular person who would have been spoilt if he had been rich. On the other hand, there are certain wealthy individuals to whom poverty is detrimental and if Allah were to impoverish them, they would go astray.

Glory be to Allah Whose mercy overwhelms His wrath. Praise and glory be to the Defender! He is Allah.

The Bringer of Harm (*ad-Darr*), the Giver of Benefit (*an-Nafi'*)

The Bringer of Harm and the Giver of Benefit are two of Allah's attributes which denote the perfection of His Supreme Power and are related to His Divine Actions. No harm or benefit can ever befall the human being save by Allah's Will: *"Say, 'Everything comes from Allah.'"* (4:78)

However, people should attribute bad things to themselves and good things to Allah, as is mentioned in the Qur'an: *"Any good thing that happens to you comes from Allah. Any bad thing that happens to you comes from yourself."* (4:79) The Prophet Ibrahim spoke with courtesy when he said, *"When I am ill, it is He who heals me"* (26:80). The following Qur'anic verse relates the episode of Musa with al-Khidr about the boat which the latter scuttled and later said, *"I wanted to damage it because a king was behind them, commandeering every boat"* (18:79); from the context it is evident that he did so in obedience to the Will of Allah: *"I did not do it of my own volition."* (18:82)

Allah – praise and glory be to Him – is the Doer of everything. He says: *"If Allah afflicts you with harm, no one can remove it except Him. If He desires good for you, no one can avert His favour. He bestows it on whomever of His slaves He wills. He is Ever-Forgiving, Most Merciful."* (10:107)

Allah – praise and glory be to Him – predetermines harm and evil for those He wills in whatever way He wishes. He impoverishes and afflicts, misleads and distresses. He bestows health, wealth, bliss, prestige, guidance and piety upon whomever He wishes, in accordance with His Wisdom and Divine Will. He predetermines all things. He is the Creator of all causes of harm, evil, good and benefit, and then distributes them as a trial: *"We test you with both good and evil as a trial, and to Us you will be returned"* (21:35); and also *"We tried them with good and evil so that perhaps they might return."* (7:168)

So Allah, the Bringer of Harm and the Giver of Benefit, has created all good and evil, harm and benefit. All these things are attributable to Him. Do not ever think that the scorpion or the snake kill with their venom on their own, or that viruses and microbes cause diseases on their own, or that food can satiate and benefit by itself, or that hunger and cold can ever take effect on their own. Do not imagine that any created thing can inflict benefit or harm by itself. All these things are merely means and causes subjected to Allah. The means and causes of harm and benefit are but the tools of Providence. He accomplishes what He wills. Nothing can ever happen except according to His Will: *"Nothing occurs, either in the earth or in yourselves, without its being in a Book before We make it happen. That is easy for Allah."* (57:22)

So nothing happens in the universe which does not accord with His Will and Plan, whether it be movement or stillness, death or life, harm or benefit, good or evil, heresy or faith, gratitude or ingratitude, gain or loss, obedience or disobedience. What He wishes happens and what He does not wish will never happen. Glory be to the Bringer of Harm and the Giver of Benefit. Praise and glory be to Him! He is Allah.

The Light (*an-Nur*)

Light is that which is manifest in itself and reveals its surroundings. The Light is one of the names of Allah, Who endows His creatures with all the spiritual and material meanings of light. Allah is the Light in every darkness, revealer of all that is hidden. He has illumined the universe with suns, stars and moons. He has lit the heavens and the earth and lit the believers' hearts with the profession of faith. He reveals Himself through His overwhelming presence and existence, brings things out from the darkness of non-existence to the light of existence. Existence itself was originally non-existent, and no darkness is more unfathomable than the abysmal darkness of non-existence.

Allah's existence was not preceded by non-existence and it is impossible for non-existence to befall Him. He is the Light. He illumines all things by giving them existence. Allah is the Light; every existence is derived and originated from His existence, and every light is derived from His Light.

Allah says: *"Allah is the Light of the heavens and the earth. The likeness of His Light is that of a niche in which there is a lamp, the lamp inside a glass, the glass as if it were a brilliant star, lit from a blessed tree, an olive, neither of the east nor of the west, its oil all but giving off light even if no fire touched it. Light upon Light. Allah guides to His Light anyone He wills and Allah makes likenesses for mankind and Allah has knowledge of everything."* (25:35) He also says: *"Allah is the Protector of those who believe. He brings them forth from darkness to the light."* (2:257) *"Is one who was dead and whom We brought to life, supplying him with a light by which to walk among people, like one who is in utter darkness, unable to emerge from it?"* (6:122) *"A Light has come to you from Allah, and a Clear Book."* (5:17)

Allah is the Light. If His Light were to be openly revealed by Him then the sublimity and the august splendour of His Countenance would annihilate all else. Glory be to the Light! Praise and glory be to Him! He is Allah.

The Guide (*al-Hadi*)

The meaning of the Arabic word *hidaya*, which means guidance, is "to gently direct to the means that lead to what is sought after". There are various kinds of guidance.

- **Guidance to the soul and innate instinct.** This makes the baby suckle its mother's breast and the chick peck its egg so that it may emerge in due time. It makes babies cry, asking to be fed or cleaned, and makes animals, when they give birth, feed and clean their children.

- **Guidance of senses and feelings.** This supplements the first. This kind of guidance is more manifest and perfect in animals, in whom it starts at an earlier age. It is also more powerful as, for instance, the sense of smell in dogs, hearing in cats, and vision in eagles and hawks.

- **Guidance of the mind.** This is granted to human beings to the exclusion of all other created beings, for which the guidance of senses and feelings suffices to mould and shape their lives and environments, as in the case of ants, bees, and the emigration of fish and birds. All these creatures are guided by instinct which is strong enough to manage their lives. But Allah endows human beings with a kind of guidance superior to the guidance of senses and instinct. It is the guidance of the mind that corrects the wrong committed by the senses and expresses its motives. If, for instance, one sees a huge thing as small at a distance or a straight bar as bent in the water, the mind corrects this information and indictates that one's distance deludes the mental faculties in estimating the size of things, that the refraction of light causes the straight bar to appear bent. It also makes one distinguish and differentiate between alternatives and contemplate what they observe in the universe, so that he can use it and try to attain a better life.

- **Guidance of religion and the Prophets.** The human mind cannot go beyond the known to the unknown or the invisible. If the mind alone were to conceive a creative power governing the universe and creating all things it might be misled into imagining that it could be the sun or the stars or that there are many gods. People are not equal as far as their mental faculties are concerned, and their awareness of the Divine truth is also different. The human mind is too imperfect to attain true knowledge of Allah. So Allah – praise and glory be to Him – imposed knowledge of Himself upon His creatures. He sent Revelation and did not leave us to rely on reasoning or imagination. He says: *"We never punish until We have sent a Messenger"* (17:15), and *"That was because their Lord would never have destroyed the cities unjustly while their people were unwarned."* (6:131)

    Allah sent His Messengers, supported them with miracles to back them up and prove their truthfulness, and sent Revelations in the form of Holy Books. Through them Allah has guided all mankind to righteous and pious deeds. Through

74

them man knows about forbidden and permitted substances and actions, hidden things such as the questions that the dead are asked in their graves, the Reckoning, the Balance, the Day of Judgement, the Narrow Bridge, Paradise, Hell, angels, jinn, Satan, and Allah's Names and Attributes and how to make supplication to Him.

- **Special guidance, or guidance directly from Allah.** This is Allah's guidance to His Prophets, Messengers and others whom He elects and selects. He blesses them and lights their way and guides their hearts to the truth. This guidance is more profound than the guidance of religion and the Prophets, which shows every human being the parting of two roads, one leading to destruction and the other to salvation. Every human being must decide which way to go – whether their ultimate fate will either be Paradise or Hell. But Allah's special guidance and gifts are selective. He taught us at the beginning of the Qur'an to ask Him in every prayer to guide us to the Straight Way: *"Guide us on the Straight Path, the Path of those whom You have blessed."* (1:6-7)

These five kinds of Divine guidance from Allah are mentioned in the Qur'an. He says: *"Our Lord is He Who gives each thing its created form and then guides it"* (20:50); *"He who determined and guided"* (87:3); and *"Had We so willed We could have given guidance to everyone."* (32:13) Allah also says: *"We guided him on the Way, be he thankful or unthankful"* (76:3); *"You are not responsible for their guidance, but Allah guides anyone He wills"* (2:272); *"You cannot guide those you love, but Allah guides those He wills"* (28:56); *"Who has more right to be followed: he who guides to the truth, or he who cannot guide unless he is guided?"* (10:35); *"But if I am guided, it is by what my Lord reveals to me. He is All-Hearing, Close-at-hand"* (34:50); *"That is the Book with no doubt. In it is guidance for the godfearing"* (2:2); *"But your Lord is enough as a guide and helper"* (25:31); and *"They are the ones whom Allah has guided."* (6:90)

All these kinds of guidance are Allah's grace and favour. Praise and glory be to the Guide! He is Allah.

The Originator (*al-Badi'*)

Al-Badi' is derived from the Arabic word *bada'a,* which means "to originate in an unprecedented way". Allah – praise and glory be to Him – is the Originator. He originated the heavens and the earth and created them in an unprecedented way. He says: *"He is the Originator of the heavens and the earth. How could He have a son when He has no wife?"* (6:101) Allah is the only Originator, Who existed before anything existed: *"He is the First. "* (57:3)

Allah originated and perfected the forms of His created beings. Nothing can match His Essence, His Attributes or His Actions. He is the Originator, eternally and permanently. Glory be to the Great Originator Who originated all created things and revealed the marvels of His creation. Praise and glory be to the Originator! He is Allah.

The Everlasting (*al-Baqi*)

The Arabic word *baqa* means "to continue to last for ever". Allah is the Everlasting Who has everlasting existence. He says: *"But the Face of your Lord will remain, Master of Majesty and Generosity."* (55:27) *"What is with you comes to an end, but what is with Allah goes on for ever."* (16:96) He will never perish and non-existence can never befall Him. His Existence is eternal and permanent.

He is the Everlasting One Whose existence is necessary. When His existence is projected into the future, then He has the name Everlasting, and when His existence is connected to the past, then He has the name Pre-eternal. The Everlasting is He whose existence has no end in the future. The Pre-eternal is He whose existence had no beginning in the past. All this is imolicit in the epithet "the Necessary Existent". These names apply according to the perspective of the human mind. Past and future are concepts of time which include motion and change. Motion is divided into past, present, and future. Change causes the changed to have a duration in which this change takes place. What is too exalted to change or to be in motion does not have a duration and so past or future do not apply to it.

Allah - praise and glory be to Him - existed before time. Time and change can never affect Him. He is the First and the Last, the Pre-eternal and the Everlasting. Praise and glory be to Him! He is Allah.

The Inheritor (*al-Warith*)

An inheritor is one to whom something reverts after the death of its owner. In the case of the created universe this applies to Allah - praise and glory be to Him. He is the Everlasting after the extinction of His creation. He is the Inheritor to Whom all things revert after their possessors perish. He says: *"It is We Who shall inherit the earth and all those on it"* (19:40) and *"You are the Best of Inheritors."* (21:89)

Allah inherits everything after the annihilation of all creatures. He says: *"To whom does sovereignty belong today?"* and He replies, *"To Allah, the One, the Conqueror!"* (40:16) All the claims of human beings, the delusions of the majority of people that they hold sway over the universe, will prove null and void when the real truth is revealed to them on that Day that the true and only Possessor is Allah.

As for people of insight, they are aware that Allah is the Lord of Power and Authority eternally. No one can in reality ever possess anything but He possesses everything. Allah is the Lord of the Worlds. He is the true Inheritor. Praise and glory be to Him! He is Allah.

The Guide to the Right Way (*ar-Rashid*)

Allah guides people to the Right Way. His management proceeds and reaches the zenith of perfection without ever consulting anyone. To Him all perfection is attributed. His wisdom is the greatest. His all-awareness is the most perfect. His judgement is always correct and sublime. He shows all His creatures the Right Way, to their happiness in this world and in the Hereafter.

In Arabic, the word *rushd* means "reason, rationality, and right judgement". *"...then if you perceive that they have sound judgement hand over their property to them."* (4:6) *"We gave Ibrahim his right guidance early on, and We had complete knowledge of him."* (21:51) Only Allah, *ar-Rashid*, can guide to the truth. He says*: "But as for anyone He misguides, you will find no helper for him to give him right guidance."* (18:17)

Glory be to Allah, the Guide to the Right Way, where lies all good and happiness! Praise and glory be to Him! He is Allah.

The Endlessly Patient (*as-Sabur*)

The Arabic word *sabr* denotes self-control, holding to what is dictated by reason and Divine law, and this is patience in obedience. *Sabr* also denotes self-restraint by not doing what is repugnant to the intellect and prohibited by Divine law, and this is patience in avoiding sin. Allah says: *"So wait steadfastly for the judgement of your Lord"* (52:48); *"...give good news to the steadfast"* (2:155); *"There are certainly Signs in that for every steadfast, thankful one"* (14:5); and *"Be steadfast, be supreme in steadfastness, be firm on the battlefield."* (3:200)

The Endlessly Patient, who could only be Allah, inspires patience and perseverance in His creatures. He is never provoked by the sins of His creatures and He does not hasten to punish them. He does not make haste to repay actions before their due time but predetermines and executes matters in a suitable way, all this without any hardships or anyone objecting. As for the patience of creatures, it is not free from suffering and conflict between what is dictated by the intelligence and religion, and what attracts them because of exasperation or lust.

The words of the Prophet Muhammad, may Allah bless him and grant him peace, are indeed true: "The Endlessly Patient is Allah Who, although His creatures say that He begot a child, keeps them in good health and sustains them." (*hadith*) Glory be to the Endlessly Patient. Praise and glory be to Him! He is Allah.

The Number of the Names of Allah

Allah has many names. Some say that they number three hundred, others a thousand and one. Yet others have said that there a hundred and twenty-four thousand, which is the same as the number of the Prophets. It has also been said that they are innumerable. The most acceptable statement is related in a *hadith* of the Prophet Muhammad, may Allah bless him and grant him peace, who said: "Allah has ninety-nine names: one hundred less one. He who memorises them enters Paradise." (*hadith*)

Those names are mentioned in the *hadith* in the order in which we have recorded them in this book. Some of the names are mentioned in the Qur'an and some are not. On the other hand, there are names that are mentioned in the Qur'an but are not mentioned in the *hadith*. If we also count all the names that could be mentioned as descriptions of Allah, the number of names would truly be countless.

Allah's Actions

Allah's Actions cannot be limited by ascribing motives, and yet they are too exalted to be chaotic. It is unreasonable to suppose that they could be void of wisdom. If some of this wisdom is hidden from even the most intelligent of mankind, it does not mean that it does not exist. Allah bestows knowledge in direct proportion to the degree of human need for that knowledge. The human mind should never transgress the limits which Allah has ordained for its imperfect knowledge and power. So we should look at created things, which represent the actions of the Creator, and try to attain knowledge of the Creator and His perfect Attributes through them. Even then the human mind is not supposed to delve into the Attributes of Allah to understand the nature of their connection to Him.

It is essential to know that Allah – praise and glory be to Him – is not compelled to perform any of His Actions. They are the fulfilment of His Will and His all-inclusive knowledge. He is never under compulsion to do anything.

Allah's Attributes

Attributes of the Divine Essence

These Attributes are inseparable from Allah Himself. His Will and Might are not identical with Him but are eternally linked to Him. Examples of these Attributes are His Life, Omniscience, Power, Will, Hearing, Sight, and Speech.

Attributes related to Divine Actions

These Attributes are connected to Allah's Will and Power in every time and place. The manifestation of these Attributes is still occurring now according to His Will, but the Attributes themselves are pre-eternal.

Allah – praise and glory be to Him – accomplishes all that He plans or desires. His Acts occur one after another according to His Wisdom and Will. Glory be to Him! He is Allah.

Avoiding false descriptions of Allah

Allah says: *"To Allah belong the Most Beautiful Names, so call on Him by them and abandon those who profane His Names."* (7:180)

Glory be to Allah! He is as He has described Himself in the Qur'an and as the Prophet Muhammad, may Allah bless him and grant him peace, described Him in his *hadiths*.

Using any kind of profanity in respect of the Names and Attributes of Allah is deviation from their authenticity and conception. Deviation from them may be the result of misstatement, negation, modality or analogy, for no one knows Allah except Allah.

Misstatement is to state wrongly and falsely. This includes any interpretation of the Most Beautiful Names which incorporate new meanings not linked to the accepted meanings mentioned in the Qur'an or *hadiths*.

Negating the attributes of Allah means to deny their relation to His Essence, or to claim that their accepted meanings are not correct without giving an alternative for them.

Modality is the belief that Allah's Attributes have a certain mode and that we can use the word 'how' when asking about them. No one can ever know the mode of these attributes but Allah. Praise and glory be to Him.

Analogy is the concept that Allah's Attributes are comparable to those of His creatures. Allah says: *"Nothing is like Him. He is the All-Hearing, the All-Seeing."* (42:9) This Qur'anic verse is fundamental to describing the Divine Attributes. It comprises both affirmation and negation. It negates any attempt at comparison when trying to comprehend and grasp the Divine Attributes. At the same time it specifically affirms the Hearing and Sight of Allah. So we must affirm and believe in the Divine Attributes without giving examples or using analogy.

Belief in Allah's existence is mandatory but it is prohibited to try to penetrate the nature of the His Essence. It is also forbidden to try to uncover the modality of His Attributes and we should not try to study the nature of the way in which His Attributes are connected to His Essence.

Some of our forefathers said about the Attributes: "They are as they are mentioned in the Qur'an and the *Sunna,* without any interpretation." Some later scholars said that there should be no attempt at studying the true meaning, the modality of the Essence, and that discussion must be restricted to the literal meanings of the Names and Attributes. Imam Ahmad ibn Hanbal said, "We should not attribute to Allah anything except what He has attributed to Himself or what His Prophet, may Allah bless him and grant him peace, attributed to Him, without our transgressing the Qur'an and the *hadith*." Nu'aym ibn Hammad said, "Anyone who compares Allah to His creatures is an unbeliever and anyone who denies what Allah has attributed to Himself is an unbeliever."

Metaphorical Verses

Verses that mention the Divine Attributes – such as: *"...the All-Merciful, established firmly on the Throne"* (20:5); *"All things are perishing except His Face"* (28:88); *"...so that you might be brought up under My eye"* (20:39); *"Allah's Hand is over their hands"* (48:10); and *"...the heavens are folded up in His Right Hand"* (39:67) were considered by the early believers to be metaphorical. *Hadiths* which included references to Divine traits such as "Allah laughed"; "Allah was surprised"; "Allah was glad", and "Allah descends" were considered in the same light.

The consensus of the opinion of the Imams, as well as that of Sufyan ath-Thawri, Ibn al-Mubarak, Ibn 'Uyayna, and Waki', was that one should believe in the Attributes, leave the understanding of their reality to Allah, abandon interpretation, and believe that Allah is too exalted for their literal meaning to be applied to Him since no comparison can be drawn between Allah and any created being. This accords with what Umm Salama said commenting on the verse: *"Allah, the All-Merciful, is established firmly on the Throne."* (20:5) She said, "The 'establishment' is well-known, its modality is unknowable, recognition of it is part of faith, and denial of it is unbelief."

Muhammad ibn al-Hasan said: "The scholars agreed to believe in the Attributes without interpretation or use of analogy." Many scholars have said: "We must follow the early believers who forbade discussion of the meaning of these verses." They include Ibn Taymiyya, Ibn al-Qayyim, and many others. Imam ar-Razi said: "The early scholars, along with their successors, agreed that we should abandon interpretation once the impossibility of understanding the word by its literal meaning has been demonstrated."

Some later scholars, however, have persisted in disputes to the extent that some of them declared others to be unbelievers. This is a fruitless and dangerous conflict and we pray to Allah to guard us against it and guide us to the Right Way; and He guides whom He will to the Right Way.

In the Qur'an there are certain verses in which traits of Allah are mentioned, such as: *"Allah is well-pleased with them," "The curse of Allah is upon him,"* and *"They followed that which called forth the anger of Allah."* Some have said that these traits are applicable in the perfect way that befits Him, without resembling traits of His creatures in any way. Others have said that they do not constitute attributes of Allah and should not be ascribed to Him. Names should not be derived from these traits: they are Divine Actions that have deep meanings far above any literal interpretations. For instance, satisfaction denotes reward, and wrath and indignation denote retribution.

There are also verses in which other Divine traits are mentioned, such as: *"...and your Lord arrives with the angels rank upon rank"* (89:22); and *"What are they awaiting but for Allah to come to them in the shadows of the clouds, together with the angels, in which case the matter will have been settled?"* (2:210) One group assert that these verses furnish proof of two Divine Attributes related to Divine Actions, namely the attributes of coming and of arriving. We should believe in them and avoid interpretations which inevitably lead to unbelief. The other group claim that Allah's coming in the clouds refers to His punishment. They support their argument by the fact the punishment came to the people of 'Ad from a cloud.

The first group answer that the verses are clear and leave no room for misinterpretation. This *ayat* clearly states that the unbelievers are awaiting for 'Allah to come to them in the clouds' to judge between them on the Day of Resurrection. This is clearer still in the verse *"...and your Lord arrives with the angels rank upon rank."* (89:22) This cannot possibly be construed as denoting punishment. It clearly refers to the arrival of the angels, the arrival of the Lord, and the arrival of certain Divine Signs.

They also said that the verse *"...and your Lord arrives with the angels rank upon rank"* (89:22) cannot be interpreted to mean the coming of Allah's punishment because what is clearly meant is His coming on the Day of Judgement to judge every person. It is at that time that the angels will be in ranks to show their respect for Him. When He comes, the sky will be split by clouds.

Allah – praise and glory be to Him – comes, goes, descends, approaches, and withdraws. But any attempt to understand this in a literal way will inevitably involve making a comparison between Him and His creatures and is therefore forbidden.

Allah's Face

Allah – praise and glory be to Him – says: *"But the Face of your Lord will remain, Lord of Majesty and Generosity"* (55:27) and *"All things are passing except His Face."* (28:88) Does this denote a fixed Attribute of Allah or should it be interpreted as signifying 'direction' or the Essence?

One faction holds that these two verses clearly ascribe a Face to Allah – glory be to Him – and that His Face is therefore distinct from His Essence. This does not mean that the Almighty has parts. The Face is attributed to Allah in the way that is appropriate for Him; His Face bears no resemblance to any other face and no other face resembles His in any way. In the verse Allah connects His Face to the epithet *"Lord of Majesty and Generosity"* which proves that His Face is not a synonym for His Essence but is one of His Attributes like *"Lord of Majesty and Generosity"*. The same can be said of the *hadiths*: "I invoke the protection of the light of Your Face," and "His Veil is light and if He were to unveil it the sublime splendour of His Face would annihilate His creatures' vision." (Muslim) The second verse mentioned above also ascribes permanence to the 'Face'.

Another group say that Allah's words *"But the Face of your Lord will remain, Lord of Majesty and Generosity"* (55:27) simply mean that Allah Himself is the Everlasting and the word "Face" refers to His Essence. In support of this, they state that Ibn 'Abbas said that 'Face' is used to refer to Allah Himself because "the

Everlasting" is one of the of the names of Allah: Allah will continue to exist after creation has been annihilated. Moreover it is a characteristic of Arabic grammar that words which literally mean 'face' and 'eye' are used pronominally.

Yet others say that the verse refers to the everlasting existence of the means by which a human being is able to approach Allah. The same meaning is implied in the Qur'anic verses: *"But right actions which are lasting are better in reward, in your Lord's sight, and a better basis for hope"* (18:46); and *"We feed you only out of desire for the Face of Allah."* (76:9) These words express the true goal of pious charity. The same applies to the saying of the Prophet Muhammad, may Allah bless him and grant him peace, "Anyone who builds a mosque for the Face of Allah will be granted by Allah a building similar to it in Paradise." (al-Bukhari and Muslim) This is clearly metaphorical. A further illustration of this is found in what Allah will say to the angels on the Day of Resurrection: "I shall not accept any actions other than those done out of desire for My Face."

The assertion of the first group that these verses clearly ascribe a Face to Allah which is distinct from His Essence is totally unsubstantiated. The assertion that it is an established Divine Attribute by which He turns to those He has chosen and to those who obey Him is also unfounded. They have been forced to resort to misinterpretation of Qur'anic verses to justify their position.

Comment

We should simply believe in these verses in the way that they were conveyed to us. We should not try to interpret them but should assign to Allah alone – praise and glory be to Him – the knowledge of their true meaning. He is too Exalted to bear any resemblance to any created thing. We must abandon any attempt at interpretation because it is clear that it is impossible to accept the literal meaning of the word "Face". Such was the viewpoint of our ancestors with respect to verses of this kind. Praise be to Allah! No one truly knows Him save He Himself.

Allah's Hands

Allah says: *"What prevented you from prostrating before what I created with My own Hands?"* (38:75) and *"Both His Hands are open wide."* (5:67) Does this refer to an Attribute of Allah or should it be interpreted as denoting power and benficience.

One group assert that these two Qur'anic verses are proof that Allah's Hands are a true Attribute as becomes Him – we cannot say that the word 'Hands' is simply an expression signifying might or power. Allah created everything – even Iblis – by His power. That would not leave Adam with anything special to distinguish him from other creatures. Furthermore, Allah says "two Hands": this can only denote actual hands since it is not possible to speak about "two powers" or "two beneficiences". Nor is to possible to apply "Hand" as a metaphor for power to something which does not actually have a hand. One cannot say, "The wind has a hand" or the "the water has a hand" when one alludes to their power. Such a metaphor is only used for something which has a hand.

The other group say that the word "Hand" does simply stands for might and generous giving. They point out that "Hand" is used in the Qur'an in the singular, as in *"Allah's hand is over their hands"*; in the dual, as in *"Both His hands are open wide and He gives however He wills"* (5:64;, and in the plural, as in *"Have they not seen how We created for them, by Our own hands, livestock which are under their control?"* (36:71) The Prophet Muhammad, may Allah bless him and grant him peace, said, "The Right Hand of Allah is full day and night and is never depleted by what He spends!" (*hadith*) He also said, "To the right of Allah, and both His hands are right." (*hadith*) These expressions cannot be taken according to their surface meanings, so some kind of analogical interpretation is necessary in this instance.

Allah's Eye

One group say that Allah's Eye is a true Attribute as becomes Him. Others contend that in the Qur'anic verses the word "Eye" as applied to Allah simply refers to His vision, care and surveillance. The claim that Allah praises Himself by attributing Eyes to Himself, and that it is impossible for Allah to attribute to Himself something He does not have in reality either is refuted because it implies a defect or that He - glory be to Him - needs to have eyes to see. It is care and surveillance that are meant in these verses.

Comment

There is a danger that the viewpoint of the first group might delude us into interpreting these verses in the light of corporeality or division into actual physical parts. Their opinion suggests that Allah has a Face, a Hand (or maybe two), and an Eye to see with, which in turn might cause the mind to be deluded into imagining and thinking things which would compromise Allah's sublimity, exaltation and honour. They have also been compelled to impose a literal interpretation upon the Qur'anic verses and *hadiths* which mention "face", "hand" or "eye." If we were to accept their assertion, then how do we interpret these terms when they are used in respect of some of the Prophets? Examples of this usage are *"And remember Our slaves Ibrahim, Ishaq and Ya'qub, men of true strength ('hands') and inner sight (eyes)"* (38:45) and *"Remember Our slave Da'ud, who possessed true strength (hands)."* (38:17)

Allah's "Company" (*Ma'iyya*)

Is Allah's "company" actual or metaphorical? Allah - glory be to Him - says: *"He is with you wherever you are"* (57:4); *"Do not be despondent, Allah is with us"* (9:40); *"...Allah is with you"* (47:35); *"Allah is with the steadfast"* (2:249); and *"Three men do not confer together secretly without Him being the fourth of them."* (58:7)

One group holds that Allah's "company" is general and all-inclusive, embracing all creatures. Allah Almighty accompanies everything through His Omniscience, His Power, and His all-pervading Sublimity: nothing can ever escape Him. The others assert that the "company" of Allah is metaphorical and stands for His knowledge, power, victory, and support, so in fact they agree on this point with the members of the first group.

Comment

We find that the first group adheres to the literal meaning in some instances but then objects to using the literal meaning on other occasions. They accept the literal meaning of Eye and Hand, but have resorted to interpretation in respect of Allah's "company". The other group try to interpret these things in a way which could well lead to an arbitrary and inaccurate use of language. The truth is that these Qur'anic verses and *hadiths* are metaphorical, but we should not try to delve into them or we may become among those whom Allah mentioned in the verse: *"Those with deviation in their hearts follow what is open to interpretation in it, desiring conflict, seeking its inner meaning."* (3:7) Allah decisively settles the matter by declaring: *"No one knows its inner meaning but Allah."* (3:7)

So it is our clear duty to abandon interpretation and to have faith in these verses, believing in them as the first Muslims did without trying to rationalise their meaning. Then we will be rightly guided. *"Those firmly rooted in knowledge say, 'We believe in it: all of it is from our Lord.'"* (3:7) It is impossible to compare Allah to any created thing, for nothing resembles Him. Glory be to Him! He is Allah.

The Descending of Allah

Is Allah's descending real or figurative? The Prophet Muhammad, may Allah bless him and grant him peace, said: "Allah descends to the lower heaven in the final third of the night."

One group say that Allah does descend, but in a way which befits Allah's exaltation and cannot be compared to the descent of creatures. Hence the ability to descend is a true attribute of Allah, in the manner He wishes. They argue that the Prophet Muhammad, may Allah bless him and grant him peace, told us that Allah descends but did not mention to us the manner of His Descent.

The other group holds that the Descent is not a reality but refers to the opening of the gates of repentance, mercy and answering of worshippers' prayers, since it is not permissible to think of Allah moving from one place to another because that is a characteristic of created things.

Comment

Once again we must believe in the Prophetic *hadith* as it is without trying to interpret it. It suffices us to know that it is recommended that we, wherever we are, ask for Allah's forgiveness, pray and resort to Him in the late hours of the night when everything is peaceful and there is the least chance of hypocrisy and we can direct ourselves to Allah with absolute devotion to Him.

Allah's Speech

One group say that speech can genuinely be attributed to Allah. He – glory be to Him – speaks whenever He wills by His power. Allah Almighty spoke to Musa and Adam with a voice, but His Words and Voice are an attribute of His Essence and cannot be compared to the words and the voices of creatures. He – glory be to Him – says in the Qur'an: *"And Allah spoke directly to Musa."* (4:164) Other Qur'anic verses also indicate that Allah Almighty really spoke to Musa directly and not by means of angels: *"We called out to him from the right hand side of the Mount"* (19:52) and *"When Musa came to Our appointed time and his Lord spoke to him."* (7:143) So it is clear that His Speech must have taken the form of a voice which was audible to Musa.

The Holy Books are also Allah's Speech. Allah speaks in the Torah in the Hebrew language and in the Qur'an in the Arabic tongue. His Book is inscribed both on the Preserved Tablet and in the copies of the Qur'an in this world.

The other group assert that Allah – glory be to Him – commands, forbids, warns, promises, and threatens by His Speech, which is eternal, timeless, and unparalleled and cannot be compared to the speech of His creatures. It is not uttered in a voice produced by the vibration of air or the movement of the lips and tongue. Although the Qur'an is recited by tongues, written in books, and memorised by hearts, it is timeless and eternal, deriving its existence from the Existence of Allah, and will never be dispersed, fragmented or altered in being conveyed to the human hearts or to pages. This group say that Musa heard Allah's speech without any need of a voice just as the righteous see Allah without a body in the Hereafter.

Speech is internal while voices are fragmented into letters which are used as indicators just as physical gestures can be used as indicators. That which is "timeless" designates that which is not preceded by anything. Thus in the expression, *"Bismillah"* ("In the name of Allah") the 's' cannot be timeless because it comes after the 'b'. Just as it is logical for Allah Almighty to have a single attribute of knowledge which encompasses all known things, so it is equally logical for His Essence to possess a single attribute of speech which denotes all that can be used to express something. His Speech is timeless and uncontingent, as is the case with all His Attributes. It is impossible for Allah to be subject to temporalities or change.

Thus Allah's Speech is Timeless while the voices which articulate it are and indicate it are contingent. The words of Allah *"Take off your sandals"* (20:12) have existed from before time, but that actual order was addressed to Musa after he came into existence.

Comment

Allah's Speech is well-known. The manner of its conveyance is unknowable. Belief in it is obligatory. Any attempt to delve into the subject is rebellion against the teaching of our ancestors.

We ask the first group: how did did Jibril impart Revelation to the Prophet, peace be upon him? Sometimes Jibril came to him in the form of a human being and spoke directly to him while at other times the Revelation came to him like the ringing of a bell after which he could retain what had been revealed to him. How could that Revelation have been an actual voice when his Companions who were with him heard nothing? Moreover the Prophet differentiated between the voice of Jibril when he was in human form and the Revelation when it came in the form of the ringing of a bell. In the case of the words of Allah *"We revealed to Musa's mother"* (28:6), does this mean actual physical words or merely inspiration as is seen in another verse where Allah says, *"Your Lord revealed to the bees: 'Build dwellings in the mountains and the trees, and also in the structures which men erect.'"* (16:68)

Normal human speech takes place when the lips are brought together and the tongue moves so that the sound is articulared as letters. Sounds arise from the friction and produce sound waves. This needs air because a sound cannot travel in a vacuum. That clearly is not applicable to Allah – praise and glory be to Him – so Allah has no voice in any normal understanding of the word.

On the other hand it is clear that Musa, and others, heard Allah's Speech in the form of words addressed to them. Allah Almighty said: *"And Allah spoke directly to Musa."* (4:164) So we must believe that Allah speaks; but we have to entrust the knowledge of the manner of that speech to Allah, Who is unequalled. Praise and glory be to Him! He is Allah.

Other Attributes of Allah

In some Prophetic sayings other traits are attributed to Allah – praise and glory be to Him – such as laughter, pride, disappointment, happiness and hatred, about which scholars have different opinions.

One group declare that believers should believe in everything which Allah has attributed to Himself, such as His establishment of the Throne, His coming, arrival, descent to the lower heaven, laughter, pleasure, wrath, hatred and love. We should believe in these Attributes as we believe in creation, sustenance, life and death. This belief must be devoid of any blemish, misstatement, negation, modality or analogy, so that there may be no danger of believing anything about Allah – praise and glory be to Him – which does not befit Him.

In the *hadith* where the Prophet, may Allah bless him and grant him peace, said, "Allah delights in people's repentance, and His delight is greater than the delight of a man who rejoices over finding his lost camel," the attribute of delight which is mentioned is one of the true attributes that befit Allah – glory be to Him. It is one of the attributes that are linked to His Will and Power. He rejoices over people's repentance and His delight indicates that He has accepted their repentance. Allah's delight is exalted above any comparison with the joy and the delight of any creature, in itself, its reasons or its objective. It is the perfection of His Mercy and Compassion which He wishes people to experience. Its objective is the completion and perfection of His generosity towards those who repent.

They also assert that laughter is an attribute of Allah. This attribute is mentioned in the *hadith*: "Allah laughs at two men, one of whom kills the other, and then both of them go to Paradise." His laughter does not resemble the laughter of creatures when they are happy but takes place through His Will and Might.

This group also assert that surprise is an attribute of Allah. They point out that surprise in reference to Allah does not arise from lack of foreknowledge of the causes or true state of affairs, as is the case with created beings, but it is used when the result of His Will and Wisdom is something which can properly be described as 'surprising'.

They assert that Allah has a "Foot" based on the *hadith* which says that Allah will "put His Foot into Hell." They claim that this entails that this is a Divine Attribute like other Divine Attributes, but in a manner which befits His Majesty and Sublimity.

The other group said that these expressions are not meant in their literal sense at all but refer to specific Divine Actions deriving from the Divine Volition which derives from Allah's Essence.

They say that Allah's delight with His creature denotes His desire for him to be endowed with blessings, while His anger towards someone denotes His desire for them to suffer punishment. Allah's delight is synonymous with His good pleasure which denotes the Divine Will to reward. The same applies to the various other attributes referred to.

Comment

It is clear that the traits of laughter, surprise, delight, love, hatred and anger refer to feelings and not to actions. But it is also clear that Allah's attributes are eternal and unchanging and that the kind of mood changes associated with these things cannot be attributed to Allah. Because of this our ancestors saw that we should not allow our minds to delve into metaphorical verses of the Qur'an and similar Prophetic sayings.

As we have said, it is safer and more appropriate to believe in the Qur'anic verses and the *hadiths* without interpretation or analogy. We should say, as our ancestors said, that the Qur'anic verses and the *hadiths* should be taken exactly as they came without interpretation. Only Allah knows what is truly meant by them: *"Nothing is like Him. He is the All-Hearing, the All-Seeing."* (42:9) Glory be to Him! He is Allah.

The vital importance of a correct understanding of Allah's Attributes

The Prophet Muhammad said, may Allah bless him and grant him peace, "Allah existed and there was nothing with Him. His Throne was on the water and He wrote everything on the Tablet and created the heavens and earth." He also said, "When Allah created everything, He wrote in His Book which is over His Throne: 'My Mercy precedes My Wrath.'"

The Prophet's companions accepted what he said without ever trying to work out how, why, where, or when. Their main concern was knowledge of the commands and prohibitions of Allah so that they might follow His commands and avoid His prohibitions in order to gain a reward from Him and avoid His punishment. What they could not translate into action they believed in implicitly. That was their attitude towards the Qur'an in matters which were not related to commands or prohibitions, such as stories of the former nations, hidden and unseen things.

There is no doubt that human knowledge increases day by day, sciences develop, new discoveries are made and new facts about the universe are brought to light. The Companions of the Prophet, may Allah bless him and grant him peace, and those who followed them were instructed by the Qur'an to learn from existence. *"Have they not looked at the camel, how it was created?"* (88:17) This and many other verses carry the same message.

Understanding of the verses has changed through time. Take, for instance, the verse, *"And the sun runs to its resting place. That is the decree of the Almighty, the All-Knowing."* (36:38) The Companions understood from this that what was meant was the course of the sun from the east to the west, which is visually observable. Their successors discovered that what really moves is the earth and not the sun, so they said that the Qur'anic verses were addressed to mankind and that Allah – praise and glory be to Him – therefore addressed them according to the normal human perspective. Then they have been followed by a people in our own time who know that the statement is literally true because the sun is actually moving through space pulling all the solar system to a place known only to Allah. Only He – glory be to Him – knows what will be discovered later on.

All this relates to the Actions and Attributes of Allah but our reflection must halt here because we are forbidden to reflect on the nature of Allah's Essence according to the *hadith*: "Contemplate the Attributes and Names of Allah but do not ever contemplate His Essence so that you may not be led astray." Contemplating what we are prohibited to contemplate will inevitably be detrimental to our faculties and faith.

Allah Almighty created us for a purpose and imposed on us certain duties and responsibilities. The aim of our creation is hidden from us, whereas our duties and responsibilities are perfectly and fully revealed to us. So we should not occupy ourselves in contemplating the aim of creation to the detriment of our duties and responsibilities. We should contemplate the effects of Allah's Attributes but not His Essence and its secrets.

Allah's Actions that are related to the Divine Will and Power remain as they are and should never be questioned, for Allah – glory be to Him – is the Lord and the Doer of all that He intends. We should not ask "why?" or "how?" with respect to Allah's Actions or with respect to the duties Allah has imposed upon mankind, for Allah Almighty has ordained whatever He pleases in order to differentiate between those who are obedient and those who are disobedient.

✽✻✽✻✽

There are several examples in the Qur'an of direct intervention by Allah interrupting the normal course of events. One is when Musa asks to see Allah: *"'My Lord, show me Yourself so that I may look at You!' He said, 'You will not see Me, but look at the mountain. If it remains firm in its place, then you will see Me.' But when His Lord manifested Himself to the mountain, He crushed it flat and Musa fell unconscious to the ground. When he regained consciousness he said, 'Glory be to You! I turn in repentance to You and I am the first of the believers!'"* (7:143) We can infer from this that vision of Allah is not impossible, since Allah makes it conditional on the mountain staying firm in its place – which would be possible if Allah willed it.

In this world vision is ephemeral and it is impossible for something ephemeral to see the Everlasting. But in the Hereafter the believers will be endowed with immortal bodies, everlasting delight, and eternal sight and will be able to see the Everlasting with their everlasting sight: *"Faces that Day will be radiant, gazing at their Lord."* (75:22-23) We ask Allah to grant us the bliss of seeing Him on the Day of Resurrection, and the righteous deeds we need to make it possible.

Another example is the story of 'Uzayr: *"Or the one who passed by a town which had fallen into ruin. He asked, 'How can Allah restore this to life when it has died?' Allah caused him to die a hundred years, then brought him back to life. Then He asked, 'How long have you been here?' He replied, 'I have been here a day or part of a day.' He said, 'Not so! You have been here a hundred years. Look at your food and drink – it has not gone bad. And look at your donkey – so We may make you a Sign for all mankind. Look at the bones, how We raise them up and clothe them in flesh.' When it had become clear to him, he said, 'Now I know that Allah has power over all things.'"* (2:259)

A third example is Ibrahim's request which is mentioned in the Qur'an: *"When Ibrahim said, 'My Lord, show me how You bring the dead to life.' He asked, 'Do you not then believe?' He replied, 'Indeed I do! But so that my heart may be at peace.' He said, 'Take four birds and tame them to yourself. Then put a part of them on each mountain and call them. They will come rushing to you. Know that Allah is Mighty, Wise.'"* (2:260)

And there is also Sulayman and the story of the throne of Bilqis: *"He who possessed knowledge from the Book said, 'I will bring it to you before your glance returns to you.' And when he saw it standing firmly in his presence, he said, 'This is part of my Lord's favour to test me to see if I give thanks or show ingratitude.'"* (27:40) This is a clear example of Allah giving someone access to the command "'Be!' and it is!"

All these examples show us how, if Allah wills, the normal laws of nature cease to apply, so that we may understand that in reality it is Allah's power alone that is effective in existence. We co-exist in this world with effects which Allah has in the normal course of things linked to particular causes; but in Paradise secondary causes will be eliminated, leaving the effects alone. The reality is that Allah accomplishes what He wills and nothing occurs in His Kingdom except what He wills. Praise and glory be to Him! He is Allah.

"'Be!' and it is"

Allah says: *"His command when He desires a thing is simply to say to it 'Be!' and it is."* (36:82) The moment Allah wills a thing it becomes His Word or Command and the thing at once comes into existence. But is the command to exist received in a state of existence or of non-existence? For if something does not exist, what is being commanded? And if it does exist, why is the command necessary? The answer is one of the three following alternatives:

- It is information revealed to us by Allah about the perfection of His Power over His existing creatures and the fulfilment of His Will, as in the case of His Command to the Children of Israel to be apes, despised and rejected, when they immediately became as He wished them to be. In this case the command "Be!" was not to a thing that did not exist.

- Allah knows everything that will exist before its existence and everything that will happen before it happens. So all existing things pre-existed before their actual existence in the omniscience of Allah, in the form He had predetermined for them. Then He commanded them to exist so they emerged out of non-existence into existence, from the realm of the Unseen to the realm of the seen.

- This is an all-inclusive Revelation given to us by Allah and includes everything that is created by Him. If He wills, a thing will be created even without a word being said by Him. It is the will of Allah expressed in terms of the Divine word "Be!" to represent His perfect power and its effect on what He wills, so that the Divine will is fulfilled without denial, cessation, or even the need to be an instrument.

The Word of Allah is pre-eternal and not created. All that happens only does so because Allah has willed it: good or evil, benefit or harm. If someone sees in his kingdom something he hates and does not want, this can only be because he is powerless to prevent it, something which could never apply to Allah, Who is the All-Powerful eternally. The Divine Command "Be!" emanates from the very Essence of Allah. Praise and glory be to Him! He is Allah.

The Nature of Human Action

Every human being has a certain power of discrimination between what is beautiful and ugly and is attracted to the beautiful and repelled by ugly things. This applies to sight, hearing, smell and also applies in respect of abstract things such as honesty, truthfulness, honour and valour and their opposites. So all industries have been established, civilisations developed, and discoveries made with the aim of making the life of the human being pleasanter and more comfortable.

Tastes differ, however, and many things combine both ugliness and beauty. Ugly things may also be beautified by their effect, as in the case of a bitter medicine that cures a disease, and conversely beautiful things may become ugly through their effect. These things are recognised by the human mind in its differentiation between the useful and the harmful, the good and the evil. Every human being weighs his actions by the measure of his own understanding and perception. He estimates his own actions and assesses their consequences.

Nevertheless, the consequences of his actions may not coincide with his expectations, in which case he must review the causes of his failure. If the reason for his failure is his own fault and negligence, then he will try again having learnt from the shortcomings of his previous attempt. But if he sees that the cause of his failure is beyond his power, he should realise that there exists in the universe an overwhelming Power far above his own and submit to the dictates of his destiny.

He should realise that his happiness in this world and the Next depends partly on the choice and the abilities granted to him but that Allah's Power is the source of all the powers and abilities of His creatures. Allah's Will is above the will of all created beings, and one of the effects of the Divine Will is that it can hinder a human being from fulfilling and executing his aim. Nothing can help him attain his aim save the help of Allah, Who alone holds absolute power over all the means that help or hinder a creature.

The human being may know that he must utilise all the faculties and powers Allah has endowed him with in the fulfilment of his freely chosen deeds and should learn from his mistakes and faults to attain the best possible results and as many of Allah's favours and gifts as he can. But he must know that the keys of heaven and earth are in Allah's Hands. Praise and glory be to Him Who alone expands or restricts the means of subsistence!

Knowing this a human being will expend every effort but will know that he must place total and absolute reliance on Allah. Allah is the Creator of everything, both created beings and their needs, and predetermined their lives and deaths, their subsistence and powers. Allah creates the spider and its web, bees and their honey, ants and their perseverance, the moon and its orbit, and the human being and his deeds. All organisms and everything in the heavens or on earth are created by Allah, the Originator of all existence.

Everything was ordained and recorded by Allah before creation, so since the Divine Pen recorded everything that would take place until the Day of Judgement it follows that everything that takes place must coincide with what was recorded before creation. However, although nothing in Allah's foreknowledge negates man's free will, Allah Almighty knows that a creature will do a certain deed at a certain time and will be rewarded or punished for what he did, so that what takes place in reality is nothing but the fulfilment of Allah's will.

At the same time we know that human beings' actions are the outcome of their good or evil intentions. There is a clear difference between involuntary movements such as heart-beats and breaths and voluntary movements such as moving from side to side and all actions stemming from a human being's freely taken decision to act.

So although no action can conflict with Allah's Will this does not mean that He is necessarily pleased with every act. He is not pleased that some human beings are unbelievers even though the fact that they are is not contrary to His Will. *"If Allah had willed, they would not have attributed partners to Him"* (6:107) and *"If your Lord had willed, all the people on the earth would have believed."* (10:99)

Disobedience and evil action on the part of human beings is not against Allah's Will but is certainly against His command. *"Say: 'Allah does not command indecency. Do you say about Allah what you do not know?'"* (7:28) Allah commands us to believe and to be obedient. *"Allah commands to justice and doing good and giving to relatives, and He forbids indecency, wrongdoing, and tyranny."* (16:90)

This shows that there is a difference between Allah's Command and His Will. They may coincide and they may differ. And it is vital for us to understand that in spite of its all-encompassing nature Allah's Will does not conflict with the free will of his human creatures to obey Him or disobey Him. To explain this apparent paradox Allah says in the Qur'an: *"And anyone who wills pays heed to it. But they will only pay heed if Allah wills"* (74:55-56); *"To whoever among you wills to go straight. But you shall not will unless Allah wills, the Lord of all the Worlds"* (81:28-29); and *"So whoever wills should take a Way towards his Lord. But you shall not will unless Allah wills. Allah is All-Knowing, All-Wise."* (76:29-39)

Summary

Allah Almighty created all created beings and is Aware of all their deeds. He inscribed everything along with its destiny on the Preserved Tablet in pre-eternity. Once a foetus develops to a certain stage in the uterus on its way to becoming a human being, Allah orders an angel to record four things already registered on the Preserved Tablet. These four things are: the place and time of his death, his livelihood, the details of his life, and whether he will be blessed or damned.

All the faculties and abilities of the human being are the creation of Allah Who put these powers at his disposal and enabled him to use them. Everything that takes place in His Kingdom accords with His Will. Allah permits the occurrence of evil so that the unbelievers and the sinners will have no plea against Him. If Allah admitted the unbelievers to Hell the moment they were created, their complaints would be justified. *"If We had destroyed them with a punishment before this, they would have said, 'Our Lord, why did You not send us a Messenger, so we could have followed Your Signs before we were humbled and disgraced?'"* (20:134)

Allah has ordered His creatures to be obedient. He sent Messengers who were supported with miracles and He sent the Holy Books with exact and precise instructions: *"...so that people will have no argument against Allah after the coming of the Messengers"* (4:1654); *"We never punish until We have sent a Messenger"* (17:15); and *"Your Lord would never destroy any cities without first sending to their capital a Messenger to recite Our Signs to them. We would never destroy any cities unless their inhabitants were wrongdoers."* (28:59) Nevertheless, Allah chooses whomsoever He pleases and blesses them with His success and guidance. The Almighty says: *"Allah chooses Messengers from the angels and from mankind"* (22:75); *"Your Lord creates and chooses whatever He wills"* (28:68); and *"Allah chooses for Himself anyone He wills and guides to Himself those who turn to Him."* (42:13)

Within this framework people are free to choose and act as they like but have no power to make things happen. They are called to account for their intentions, which is why the Prophet Muhammad, may Allah bless him and grant him peace, said "Actions only go by intentions, and everyone gets what they intend." Allah says: *"If anyone leaves his home, emigrating to Allah and His Messenger, and death catches up with him, it is Allah Who will reward him."* (4:100) *"Your Lord knows best what is in your selves. If you are right-acting, He is Ever-Forgiving to the penitent."* (17:25)

A human being's deeds are rewarded according to his intentions; but intentions alone are not sufficient, because any good intention not accompanied by a righteous deed is simply a delusion. A true intention is one which settles in a person's heart and denotes what he really wants to do, and which he then spares no effort to make a reality. The Prophet Muhammad, may Allah bless him and grant him peace, said, "Faith is not mere expression of hopes. Faith is what has settled in the heart and is affirmed by action. There were people who departed from this world without doing a single righteous deed and said, 'We had a hopeful opinion of Allah!' But they lied, for if they had had a hopeful opinion, they would have done righteous deeds." (Related by Ibn Hanbal)

Allah's Favour and Justice

Allah Almighty declares that He is never unjust. He says in the Qur'an: *"They will not be wronged"* (2:281); *"Allah does not want any injustice for His slaves"* (40:31); and *"Your Lord does not wrong His slaves."* (41:46) On the Day of Judgement, Allah Almighty will say: *"Today there will be no injustice"* (40:17); *"No self will be wronged in any way"* (21:47); *"We did not wrong them; rather they wronged themselves"* (16:118); *"Allah does not wrong them; rather they wrong themselves"* (3:117); and *"Your Lord will not wrong anyone at all."* (18:49)

So nothing comes from Allah but favour and impartial justice, and indeed, as we have seen, the Just is one of the Names and Attributes of Allah. His favours are abundant. He favoured all His creatures by giving them existence and sustenance. He does not benefit from the obedience of His creatures, nor is He harmed by their disobedience. All might and glory belong to Him since pre-eternity before He created the universe; and He is absolutely independent of everything in existence.

Allah imposes upon His creatures what He wishes. He admits them to Paradise through His Mercy and not because they deserve it, but if He consigns them to Hell then that will be by His justice. He will not be questioned for His actions but they will be questioned for theirs. (cf. 21:23)

One of the manifestations of Allah's mercy is that He has imposed on people that they should know and obey Him according to clear laws and Revelation and not according to their own mental endeavours. For this reason He sent Messengers and supported them with miracles that confirmed their truthfulness. He sent the Holy Books with clear instructions in them to reveal the Straight Path to human beings and show them the way to salvation.

Then Allah's mercy overwhelmed existence for the last time and He sent the Seal of the Prophets and gave him the Noble Qur'an which abrogated all previous religions and Divine dispensations and replaced them with the faith of Islam. The testimony "There is no god but Allah" became insufficient unless it was accompanied by the testimony that "Muhammad is the Messenger of Allah." Therefore we find that in the Final Revelation and its total implementation in the life and words of the Last Messenger, Muhammad, we have the most complete possible exposition of what can said and known about the nature of the Divine Unity, Allah, the Lord of all the worlds, and how we as human beings should act in the light of that knowledge.

He is Allah – there is no god but Him. He is the Knower of the Unseen and the Visible. He is the All Merciful, the Most Merciful. He is Allah – there is no god but Him. He is the King, the Most Pure, the Perfect Peace, the Trustworthy, the Safeguarder, the Mighty, the Compeller, the Supremely Great. Glory be to Allah above all they associate with Him. He is Allah, the Creator, the Maker, the Giver of Form. To Him belong the Most Beautiful Names. Everything in the heavens and earth glorifies Him. He is the Mighty, the All-Wise. (59:22-24)

Allah. There is no god but Him, the Living, the Self-Sustaining. He is not subject to drowsiness or sleep. Everything in the heavens and the earth belongs to Him. Who can intercede with Him except by His permission? He knows what is before them and behind them. But they cannot encompass any of His knowledge save what He wills. His Footstool encompasses the heavens and the earth, And their preservation does not tire Him. He is the Most High, the Magnificent. (2:253-254)

Everything in the heavens and the earth glorifies Allah. He is the Almighty, the All-Wise. The sovereignty of the heavens and the earth belongs to Him. He gives life and causes to die. He has power over everything. He is the First and the Last, the Outward and the Inward. He has knowledge of everything. It is He Who created the heavens and the earth in six days, then settled Himself firmly on the Throne. He knows what goes into the earth and what comes out of it, what comes down from heaven and what goes up into it. He is with you wherever you are. Allah sees whatever you do. The sovereignty of the heavens and the earth belongs to Him. Everything returns to Allah. He makes the night merge into day and the day merge into night. He knows what all hearts contain. (57:1-6)

Say: He is Allah, Absolute Oneness. Allah the Everlasting Sustainer of all. He has not given birth and was not born. And no one is comparable to Him. (112:1-4)

DAR AL TAQWA LTD

Publishers
Booksellers
Distributors
Printers & Stationers

BOOKS PUBLISHED BY DAR AL TAQWA LTD.

TITLE		NO.PAGES	PRICE
1. THE MIRACLES OF THE QURAN By Sheikh M. Al-Sharawi ISBN 1 870582 01 2	HBK PBK	276 276	£12.95 £6.50
2. THE SIGNS BEFORE THE DAY OF JUDEGEMENT By Ibn Kathi ISBN 1 870582 03 9	PBK	96	£3.95
3. THE JINN IN THE QURAN AND THE SUNNA By Mustafa Ashour ISBN 1 870582 02 0	PBK	66	£3.95
4. THE ISRAA AND MIRAJ THE PROPHET'S NIGHT JOURNEY AND ASCENT INTO HEAVEN By Abdul Hajjaj ISBN 1 870582 06 3	PBK	56	£3.95
5. THE SOUL'S JOURNEY AFTER DEATH By Layla Mabrouk ISBN 1 870582 05 5	PBK	40	£2.95
6. YASIN AND AL-RAHMAN TRANSLATED + TRANSLITERATED ISBN 1 870582 00 5	PBK	44	£1.50
7. PART THIRTY OF THE HOLY QURAN ARABIC, TRANSLATED AND TRANSLITERATED ISBN 1 870582 00 5	PBK	102	£1.95
8. **JEWELS OF GUIDANCE** By Hamza M. Salih Ajjaj ISBN 1 870582 00 4	PBK	88	£3.95
9. THE WORLD OF THE ANGELS By Sheikh Abdul Hamid Kishk ISBN 1 870582 00 6	PBK	96	£3.95
10. FATE AND PREDESTINATION By Sheikh M. Al-Sharawi ISBN 1 870582 07 1	PBK	80	£3.95
11. DIALOGUE WITH AN ATHEIST By Mustafa Mahmoud ISBN 1 870582 09 8 (Published May 1994)	PBK	180	£5.50

7A Melcombe Street, Baker Street, London NW1 6AE
Telephone: 0171-935 6385 Facsimile: 0171-224 3894
E-mail: dar.altaqwa@btinternet.com

DAR AL TAQWA LTD

Publishers
Booksellers
Distributors
Printers & Stationers

TITLE		NO.PAGES	PRICE
12.THE INTERPRETATION OF DREAMS By Ibn Sirin ISBN 1 870582 08 X (Published May 1994)	PBK	160	£5.95
13. HOW ALLAH PROVIDES By Sheikh M. Al-Sharawi ISBN 1 870582 10 1 (Published June 1994)	PBK	96	£3.95
14. MAGIC AND ENVY By Sheikh M. Al-Sharawi ISBN 1 870582 11 X (Published July 1994)	PBK	78	£3.95
15. GOOD AND EVIL By Sheikh M. Al-Sharawi ISBN 1 870582 25 X (Published August 1994)	PBK	74	£3.95
16. THE LAWS OF MARRIAGE IN ISLAM By Sheikh M. Rif'at Uthman ISBN 1 870582 30 6 (Published March 1995)	PBK	104	£4.95
17. THE ISLAMIC WILL By Hajj Abdal Haqq + Aisha Bewley Ahmad Thomson ISBN 1 870582 35 7 (Published April 1995)	PBK	68	£5.95
18. DEALING WITH LUST AND GREED **ACCORDING TO ISLAM** By Sheikh 'Abdul al-Hamid Kishk ISBN 1 870582 40 3 (Published June 1995)	PBK	145	£5.95
19. TEACH YOUR CHILDREN TO LOVE **OF THE PROPHET** By Dr. Muhammad Abdu Yamani ISBN 1 870582 45 4 (Published June 1995)	PBK	76	£3.95
20. THE WATER OF ZAM ZAM By Muhammed Abd al Aziz Ahmad Majdi as-Sayyid Ibrahim ISBN 1 870582 55 1 (Published March 1996)	PBK	53	£3.95

7A Melcombe Street, Baker Street, London NW1 6AE
Telephone: 0171-935 6385 Facsimile: 0171-224 3894
E-mail: dar.altaqwa@btinternet.com

DAR AL TAQWA LTD

TITLE		NO.PAGES	PRICE
21. PORTRAIT OF HUMAN PERFECTION By Shaykh Ahmad Muhammad Al-Hawfi ISBN 1 870582 50 0 (Published March 1996)	PBK	128	£5.95
22. YAJUJ AND MAJUJ Muhyi-d-din Abd Al-Hamid ISBN 1 870582 60 8 (Published Novermber 1996)	PBK	41	£3.95
23. MUHAMMED (SAW) Dr. Mustafa Mahmoud ISBN 1 870582 70 5 (Published March 1997)	PBK	68	£3.95
24. AL MAHDI AND THE END OF TIME Muhammed ibn Izzat Muhammed Arif ISBN 1 870582 75 6 (Published May 1999)	PBK	74	£3.95
25. THE DAY OF RISING Laila Mabrouk ISBN 1 870582 85 3 (Published September 1997)	PBK	183	£5.95
26. DUNYA THE BELIEVERS PRISON, THE UNBELIVERS PARADISE Muhammad Abd Ar Rahman Iwad ISBN 1 870582 802 (Published October 1997)	PBK	160	£5.95
27. CIRCUMCISION IN ISLAM Abu Bakr Abdu'r Razzaq ISBN 1 870582 95 0 (Published August 1998)	PBK	120	£5.95
28. JOURNEY THROUGH THE QURAN THE CONTENT & CONTEXT OF THE SURAS Muhammad al-Ghazzali ISBN 1 870582 90 X (Published August 1998)	HBK	580	£25.00
29. PART 29TH OF THE QURAN ARABIC, TRANSLATED & TRANSLITERATED ISBN 1 870582 11 X (Published October 1998)	PBK	128	£2.95

7A Melcombe Street, Baker Street, London NW1 6AE
Telephone: 0171-935 6385 Facsimile: 0171-224 3894
E-mail: dar.altaqwa@btinternet.com

DAR AL TAQWA LTD

Publishers
Booksellers
Distributors
Printers & Stationers

TITLE		NO.PAGES	PRICE
30. PART 28TH OF THE QURAN ARABIC, TRANSLATED & TRANSLITERATED ISBN 1 870582 16 0 (Published October 1998)	PBK	96	£2.96
31. DIVINE EXISTENCE VERSUS DOUBT Shaykh Muhammad M.\al-Sha'rawi ISBN 1 87 0582 26 8 (Published February 1999)	PBK	64	£3.95
32. THE HEART & THE TONGUE THEIR SICKNESSES AND CURES Sheikh Yassin Roushdy ISBN 1 870582 21 7 (Published February 1999)	PBK	48	£3.95
33. ALLAH THE DIVINE NATURE Yassin Roushdy ISBN 1 870582 31 4 (Published February 1999)	PBK	120	£5.95

7A Melcombe Street, Baker Street, London NW1 6AE
Telephone: 0171-935 6385 Facsimile: 0171-224 3894
E-mail: dar.altaqwa@btinternet.com